jon jory's
PRACTICAL ACTING

Smith & Kraus

A Smith and Kraus Book
PO Box 564, Hanover, NH 03755
editorial 603.643.6431 To Order 1.877.668.8680
www.smithandkraus.com

PRACTICAL ACTING: A TOOL KIT FOR THE HIGH SCHOOL AND COLLEGE ACTOR Copyright © 2019 by Jon Jory

All rights reserved.

Manufactured in the United States of America

CAUTION: Professionals and amateurs are hereby warned that the material represented in this book is subject to a royalty. It is fully protected under the copyright laws of the United States of America, and of all countries covered by the International Copyright Union (including the Dominion of Canada and the rest of the British Commonwealth), and of all countries covered by the Pan-American Copyright Convention and the Universal Copyright Convention, and of all countries with which the United States has reciprocal copyright relations. All rights, including professional, amateur, motion picture, recitation, lecturing, public reading, radio broadcasting, television, video or sound taping, all other forms of mechanical or electronic reproductions such as information storage and retrieval systems and photocopying, and the rights of translation into foreign languages, are strictly reserved.

ISBN: 978-1-57525-940-6
Library of Congress Control Number: 2019943284

Typesetting and layout by Elizabeth E. Monteleone
Cover design by Larry Silverberg

For information about custom editions, special sales, education and corporate purchases, please contact Smith and Kraus at editor@smithandkraus.com or 603.643.6431.

To Marcia, the love of my life

To Marcus, the love of my life

Table of contents

Foreword   9
    by Don Corathurs

Part I

1. The noble profession   13
2. Getting the best from your acting teacher   17
3. Practical acting   21
4. Acting in musicals   25
5. Working with the Director   31
6. C'est moi! The character   41
7. Acting problem number 1   45
8. The back and forth   49
9. Between the lines   53
10. The walking dead   57
11. Things people do   61
12. Taking stage   67
13. The right touch   71
14. Moving parts   75
15. The set is to do   81
16. Why I hate emotions!   85

17. The over-clarifying, too emphatic, psychologically
    one-note, terrible, horrible, no good actor   91
18. What to do when things go badly   95

PART II PERSPECTIVES ON ACTOR TRAINING

19. The conversation   101
20. Do your homework   107
21. What now?   113
22. An argument for democratic casting   117

PART III GETTING WORK AND OTHER PROFESSIONAL CONSIDERATIONS

23. What are they thinking   125
24. How do you feel?   129
25. Surviving the audition   133
26. Competitive spirit   137
27. Shakespeare acting for Philistines   141
28. Charisma   145
29. Artist in waiting   149

Foreword

When you edit a magazine you get a lot of story ideas pitched at you over the phone. It's surprising how few of them make you glad you took the call. Every now and then, though, a caller will say, in effect, "I'm going to write a series of articles that gives your readers exactly what they need and want. They will mark these articles up with highlighter, share them with their friends, quote them to their teachers, tack them to their walls. We'll do about thirty of them over the next four years and when we're done we'll make them into a book."

That's the call I got one day in 2012 from Jon Jory, distinguished director, playwright, champion of new work, and acting teacher. What he was proposing was something that did not at that time exist: a book those young actors—high school and college students—could use to shape and refine their craft. It would ground actors in the strategic fundamentals of the work and also equip them with elements of tactical nuance that give a character definition and texture.

A smart editor knows when to say yes. The first of the twenty-nine compact essays on acting in this volume appeared in the September 2013 issue of *Dramatics*. Jon's "On Acting" column ran monthly through May 2017.

Dramatics is published by the Educational Theatre Association for its members, including thousands of high school theatre students. Jon's work matched up nicely with the magazine's editorial brief, which contemplates as a first principle giving students the tools they need to become better theatre artists. (We also try to help students decide whether they want to pursue a life in the arts, and to prepare them, whether they become actors, cops, or pastry chefs, for a lifelong relationship with the theatre.)

Jon's teaching is fresh and contemporary and marinated in a wry, cheerful sense of humor. He is also reassuringly Old School. (Surely he is one of the last professional writers in the Western Hemisphere to submit his copy handwritten on a legal pad.)

Jory-trained actors start in the familiar American way with objective and given circumstances, but these ideas are enriched and embellished with nuggets of wisdom and little technical apps drawn from experience. It's an approach that Jon calls "practical acting," a way of applying real solutions to real problems. A typical example: in the chapter titled "What to Do When Things Are Going Badly," the answer is basically find the smallest wrong thing you can find, and fix that. Then find the next one. Short summary of Jon's counsel: "Try stuff."

A scan of chapter titles reveals the book's reach, which ranges across the rehearsal schedule from auditions to opening night and beyond. How to use variable rhythms to make your work more interesting. How to get along with your director. How to work between the lines with your scene partner. How to use touch to wake up a scene. Put it all together and you've got a living character.

"Let's pretend it's not mysterious and poetic," Jon writes. "Let's pretend it's more like designing a toaster..." That is a contrarian idea that becomes a comic one when Jon's students turn out toasters filled with mystery and poetry.

—*Don Corathers*

I.
PRACTICAL ACTING

1.
Practical Acting

1. The noble profession

The naysayers are always trying to talk us out of an acting career. The main point is always financial, as in "It's hard to make a living as an actor." Indeed. But if you are passionate and talented, you shouldn't allow yourself to be deterred. As the famous hockey player Wayne Gretzky once said, "You miss one hundred percent of the shots you don't take."

Here are five of the best things about being an actor.

1. A creative life. There are millions upon millions of people doing jobs they could do in their sleep. To be fully engaged and challenged by what you do is almost a definition of happiness. In acting, anything could happen at any time. As Theodore Roosevelt said, "I insist on being surprised by my day." The actor is confronted by choosing between alternatives in each moment. It is a life of the applied imagination. Onstage, in rehearsal, and while you're doing the dishes, new ideas about the role and the play pass in review. You are making what has never before existed, your vision and instinct for Hamlet and Juliet. What an unbelievable treat.
2. You dance with Shakespeare, Moliere, and Sondheim. The greatest writers lie imprisoned in their own words until you set them free in your performance. Shakespeare can't do it without you. Isn't that remarkable?

Your imagination and Shakespeare's become one thing when the curtain rises. A bit different than a career at Walmart or Toyota, eh? It is, in fact, the anti-corporate life, and one in brilliant company. You live literature. You are the story and the song. You live for hours in the worlds created by the best of us.

3. They pay you to be a storyteller. They pay you! You, in a sense, embody the wisdom and history of the tribe. Tolstoy's immortal question about life, "What then must we do?" is answered by the tales the storyteller tells. And who doesn't love stories? The crowds are always around the storyteller longing for the tale. Plays teach us both how to live and how not to live, the storyteller has always been, and is now, the crucial profession we cannot do without. Let's have no more talk about whether the actor is important to the society. Those who do not understand the past are doomed to repeat it, right?

4. The applause. It may sound callow but it is not. Applause is the sound of being appreciated. Remind me, how many jobs have that kind of appreciation built in? And why? Why is there this tradition of applause? Because the audience recognizes the level of difficulty and celebrates it. When you are acting, you are doing a difficult, even frightening thing. You are acrobats of the mind and spirit. You stand up there, unarmed, and tell it like it is. More importantly you live through how it is, so the audience may better understand their own lives. They see you do this unguarded, intimate, brave examination of a human soul right in front of them. No wonder they applaud, and no wonder you deserve it.

5. You get to play dress up. Really. You get to dress up in other people's lives, emotions, and mindsets. One grave difficulty in life is that it's hard not to get bored with

yourself. And the actor, when this almost unavoidable condition sets in, goes down to the theatre, sits down at a dressing table, and blithely slips into another life. Not only that but everyone around you has agreed you're Napoleon! And out of this impersonation comes learning. The theatre is a great education, and you don't have to live in the dorm. Every project demands research, and you can't live an actor's life without improving your understanding of history, religion, architecture, philosophy, psychology, and on and on (okay, okay, I can't vouch for your math skills). Acting is an Ivy League education.

* * *

So that's five; another twenty-five would be easy to write if we had the space. Acting is a noble profession that makes this a better world to live in, and on top of that, it's fun. I've never laughed harder than I have in rehearsal. And my private suspicion about why acting is sometimes not as well paid as it should be is that someone let the cat out of the bag about just how much fun it is and the secret cabal that runs the world decided we'd do it no matter how much it paid us. Now, that still needs fixing. Tell me when you've fixed it.

2. Getting the best from your acting teacher

A truism: You can get a little from your acting teacher or you can get a lot. You pick.

Second truism: There are wonderful, good, and indifferent acting teachers. (Surprise!) Deduction: Whatever and whoever the acting teacher might be, you want to drain them of knowledge like a glass of water in Death Valley, right?

Rule number one. You're serious about acting so let the teacher see that. Teachers want everyone to learn but they can't help being interested in the student who *really* wants to learn. You're that student, so let your interest shine like a good deed in a naughty world. Or something.

Woody Allen once observed that "eighty percent of success is showing up." Teachers have egos. They give a little bit extra to the students who feed those egos by showing up and, conversely, a little less to those who don't. Be there. Get the little more.

Rule number two. Get up and do it. Acting is experiential. Most of the learning comes from the doing. The fact of the classroom is that there probably isn't time for everyone to do the exercise or scene in that day's class. Stage time is crucial to the actor. Grab it.

When I say, "All right, who wants to go first?" over 90 percent of the actors in the class don't volunteer. See this as the golden opportunity that it is. "Stage time is available and it's going to waste. Gimme!" Why aren't people getting up? Actor fear. They don't want to make mistakes. Big mistake! You can only learn by making mistakes. You probably have 40,000 mistakes to make before you're a good actor, so you better get up and start making them. Not doing it well is the crucial first step in doing it well.

Actor fear is the veil obscuring your talent and slowing down your growth. John Guare, the famous playwright, has said that we all have a tiny, obnoxious editor living in a little room in our foreheads. We should reach up, open the tiny door, take out the tiny editor, and throw it in the wastebasket. (Well actually he said "crush it.") Let's simplify all this: get up and act!

Rule number three. Acting classes are, first of all, too large for you to get sufficient feedback on your work. In my last teaching job I usually had a two-hour class with sixteen students. That means if I see everyone's work I have a little over seven minutes per student to talk about it. You are not going to get as much as you should from me in seven minutes. Plus, we teachers like to talk, so a lot of time is spent on general principles, not individual critique.

How can you get your needs addressed? Make an appointment with me. The fact of the matter is that the teacher does not have time outside class to give individual attention to every student. The good news is that very few students ask. So ask.

Now the problem is how to get the best from the short time the acting teacher agrees to spend with you privately. Walking in and sitting there like a silent ox awaiting feed corn isn't going to work. Frankly, I haven't been burning the midnight oil thinking about your work. I've been watching *CSI: Toledo.* So come in with three questions about your work. Not eleven, three.

Here are some suggestions:

1. Do I have any speech or articulation problems I should be working on?
2. Should I be doing more physically?
3. How can I get more involved with the other actor on stage?

If you don't ask these three, ask something specific, a question to which there is a specific answer. Vague questions make the teacher wish you would vaporize or become a shoemaker on another planet.

Somewhere in the middle of answering your questions, your teacher may suddenly be struck by an insight concerning your work and take the conversation in an entirely different direction. Excellent. A side benefit to the meeting is that the teacher may be more aware of you in class and increase the feedback you hunger for.

If the teacher says he or she has no time to meet with you, wait a month and ask again. No? Wait a month and ask a third time. Very few teachers have the iron nerve to deny you three times. If they do, fuhgeddaboudit, it's not going to happen.

Rule number four. Work outside class so your in-class work is good enough to engage the teacher. Identify the classmates who are also serious about their work and try to get paired with them on class projects. They'll go the extra mile with you. Working on a monologue? Get a classmate to look at it and give you feedback, and then return the favor. Working on a scene? Fight to work with someone you admire. Try to work two one-hour sessions, minimum, outside class before you show the scene. Your work is a metaphoric iceberg and only the visible tip is, the class work. Teachers can tell if you've worked on the scene, and frankly, those who do get more attention. Remember the equation that leads to teacher involvement has to do with the work you put in. More work almost always means an increase in the acting teacher's involvement. You are never in enough acting classes to ensure your full development. For heaven's sake don't waste the one you have.

Rule number five. Ask for a reading list. Do the reading and ask for a meeting to discuss it. You know the drill. Bring three questions. Then ask if the teacher has time to look at your new audition piece.

Acting is your dream. To have the dream you have to get better. Pursue "better" actively. Don't just sit there.

3. Practical acting

Yes, yes I know acting is an "art" and as such is mysterious, poetic, metaphoric, creative, and very, very, very complicated, difficult to understand, and almost impossible to do. This being the case, it scares everybody trying to learn it and, naturally, being afraid of it makes it truly impossible to do.

So let's pretend it isn't mysterious and poetic. Let's pretend it's more like designing a toaster that does a good job toasting and is kind of nice to look at. Do these things (anybody can do them) and guess what, you'll be better at this acting thing and you won't continually have your underwear in a poetic twist.

1. Once you have gotten over the fabulous thrill of being announced on the cast list, go into your room (if you have a room, otherwise go into somebody else's room) and read the play three times. In between the readings you are allowed to eat Twizzlers, play dodge ball, etc. Is it boring to read the play over and over? Probably, but a lot about acting is boring, which your acting teacher forgot to tell you. Actually much of it is as boring as European history. Now, when you think you are ready, make somebody who likes you or is very patient sit down and eat chips and dip while you tell them, in great detail, the story of the play. From beginning to end. Clearly and, if possible, in complete sentences. If

you go into rehearsal without being able to do this, Zeus will hurl a thunderbolt at you and you will be reduced to a handful of actor-ashes. No, don't ask why, just do, it.

2. Learn your lines. This is murderously boring. Too bad. I don't mean *sort of* learn your lines. I mean be word perfect. Do this before the first day of the second week of rehearsal. If learning lines perfectly is too much work then you don't have the will and drive to be an actor or, unfortunately, almost anything else, so make sure you have a trust fund.

3. Now you know your lines and the story of the play and you are way ahead of the curve. Now you are going to have to act, but that actually isn't very complicated. Do not tell your acting teachers this because it will make them very defensive, even cranky. There are only three or four things you need to practice to be a perfectly passable actor. The first and most important one is to want something. You want something all day long. I just got tired of writing this so I wanted something to eat. Actually I wanted something sweet and I looked in the three places something sweet would be but to no avail. That forced me to the fridge, but it was either leftover kale or leftover salad. I started feeling an emotion, which I hadn't planned. It was annoyance. There were a couple of spoonfuls of soy vanilla ice cream in the freezer compartment but we all know soy ice cream is nasty. Finally I remembered there was a bag of brown sugar down with the flour and baking soda so I got it out and ate three spoonfuls. That satisfied the "eating" want, so then I "wanted" to get this in the mail by three o'clock so *Dramatics* magazine wouldn't be mad at me and now I'm writing. You need to continually want something all the time you are on stage. When you aren't

wanting something your acting sucks.

4. So, you've got the "wanting" part of acting, which is making you look pretty good, even sexy. Now this "want" has to take place within the circumstances. Let's say you dropped your keys when you were out walking your three-legged bloodhound named Sherlock. You have to have them to get back in the house, so you retrace your steps and search, but remember, it's raining. If you have a hard time remembering what rain is, go into the shower fully dressed, drop a grain of uncooked rice on the shower floor, turn on the shower and look for it. The "want" takes place in the circumstances. So if you put the "want" and the "circumstances" together, a lot of the time, you are already a pretty good actor and people will pay you. As a matter of fact, you're almost through with having to "learn" to act.

5. Number five is something you don't have to do: have emotions. If you are pursuing the "want" in the "circumstances" you will either have emotions or you won't. If you don't, the acting will still be good and you don't have to pretend to have emotions, which is as bad as soy ice cream. If emotions show up while you are looking for your keys, that's good too but don't count on it and don't try to make sounds as if you were having an emotion.

6. The last thing is the most neglected in American acting. Variety. Anything you do repetitively makes you boring and puts the audience to sleep. Well, they probably needed the sleep anyway. To this end (and don't tell anybody I said this, because the acting philosophers will get upset and drive me out of the theatrical community with flaming torches) you have to talk quickly some of the time and slowly some of the time. You have

to talk loudly some of the time and softly some of the time. You have to be very energetic some of the time and passive some of the time. You need to talk steadily some of the time and take pauses some of the time. You need to gesture some of the time and stand still some of the time. Because you know the story, want something in the circumstances, and know the lines, you can pretty much figure out, or even intuit, which part of this variety should be present in the moment, but this is not optional, you have to have the variety.

Okay, that's it. That's practical acting. There are bells and whistles you will pick up along the way, but you'll be fine for now. So stop agonizing and being afraid to get up in class or worrying if you have talent. You may find out along the way that you don't have enough talent, but that will just force you into a profession that will pay you enough to own a used Toyota. And stop worrying about "acting." The worry is having you forget the practical stuff I just told you. And remember to go fully dressed into the shower. That's a really important part. And when you meet people who say acting is really, really complicated, go into the kitchen and eat three teaspoons full of brown sugar.

4. Acting in musicals

The age-old question: is the art of acting different in musicals and plays? A more interesting question might be: will actors who primarily act in musicals like the answer to the question? Let's first answer the overall question. Obviously, musical actors need more skills, and more skills are harder than fewer skills, right? Question answered, we can all go home now.

But...

Let's leave out the most interesting acting the musical actors get to do, which is interpreting and delivering the songs. To be frank, the songs are usually the most complex text the musical actor gets to work with—rich, complicated, and emotional in both lyric and melody. There is no comparable parallel for the straight-play actor except the big poetic speeches in Shakespeare, and even there they aren't dancing at the same time. "To be or not to be" is not ordinarily a tap number.

So...

Let's stick to the musical books, where the musical actor and the play actor could be most easily compared. Here, I can semi-confidently say the acting often differs, and there are differences in approach and product. All right, the basics are the same.

1. Belief in the circumstances and situation
2. The playing of objectives (what you want)
3. Clearly telling the scene's story

However...

Musicals are very often played in larger houses, because they cost more to produce than straight plays and thus need to attract larger audiences to offset the cost. The size of the theatre impacts the actor in two ways. The show is completely miked, both for dialogue and songs, and miked acting has different necessities, including the devastating one that everything is likely to sound the same, which might be charitably said to ruin the acting. A crucial point for actors is that their job is to make the important parts of the text sound different than the less important parts. Enough, I think, said.

I once directed *Brigadoon* in an outdoor theatre seating eleven thousand. I watched from the last row. The actors were the size of my little finger's nail. The producer, seeing my confusion and dismay, told me to think of it as "a radio show with dances," which didn't really help but did assist my humility. The only point necessary to the acting was to make sure the dialogue was clear. I hated it. I hated everything about it. I'm sure by now that theatre has giant screens like games in the NFL, but I'm too old to call that "live theatre." At least in ancient Greece the actors wore masks and needed to develop powerful voices that could be heard, which I will grant as an acting skill.

Thus . . .

If you are miked for the dialogue scenes in a musical, "rate" and "vocal variety" become more important than in other forms of acting. Additionally in very large houses, gesture needs added size and ferocious intent. Large gesture takes the actor further away from realism and thus is a style all its own. Good musical actors feel more at home with this physical excess, and need to. The body needs greater freedom and creativity. The focus shifts from the eyes and expression to the body and its expression.

Now...

There are subtler differences in the dialogue scenes because of the difference in the shape of the storytelling. The dialogue scene is obviously shorter because we are moving toward a song or dance number or coming out of one.

A digression...

People do not come out of musicals humming the dialogue scenes. They are a necessary evil and sometimes a bit more if they are funny and better still if they embody physical comedy. Dialogue is an important connective tissue and moves story forward but it is neither heart nor soul.

Back to the point...

So what is special and different for the musical actor handling dialogue? Make sure the plot points are clear and clearly delivered so that the story holds. Don't take too many pauses. The material is not usually emotionally dense enough to need many. Keep the energy up, unless it is "the quiet moment" that musicals try to find a place for.

The energy...

Here's a big difference in musical acting: the energy! Coming out of a musical number there has been a lot of sound. There's the orchestra, for one thing, which is a big decibel level, plus miked singing and dancing feet on a hard surface. If the actor follows this hoopla in an ordinary speaking tone it can feel... well... depressive, making the audience actively long for the next number.

More energy, vocal and physical, and energy more sustained is demanded than in a play. Not every actor has this kind of vocal energy. Do you? If you do, to back it up you need an energetic commitment to our old friend: the want. What you need and must have in the moment. Because musical energy not backed up by commitment to the objective seems random or worse.

Other stuff...

Distinctiveness. We can't wait around in a musical for you to reveal what and who you are. Personality is a crucial player in musicals. You need the "bigs." If you are the love interest, you need big charm and often big beauty, male and female. We don't want to gradually love you. We want to love you right away! If you are the comic, you need a personality that is funny right away. We don't want to wait too long for the character to develop, because there aren't that many pages of dialogue to develop you. Dialogue scenes in musicals tend to be plot-focused, not character-focused. The actor needs this distinct personality from the moment the overture ends. These kinds of personalities are not usually developed in drama schools. You've had it since you were four.

Size...

Musical performances tend to be bigger than life (not always but mainly), and the actor who is comfortable with this larger size is the actor who tends to flourish in musicals. Size of the work can be developed as opposed to size of personality, which can't. I could usually point out the musical actors in a high school or undergraduate acting program (and have) by watching their personalities at work in the hallway.

To close...

The basics of all acting are the same, whether it's in commercials or opera, but the acting (dialogue) in musicals demands extra doses of personality, plot skills, energy, distinctiveness, comic skills, and type. Somebody should write the book.

5. Working with the director

There's one constant in a working actor's life: the director. Working well with the director is part of the actor's art. What are the dos and don'ts? What's the psychology of such a relationship? How can you, the actor, get the most out of the rehearsal period? Let us make a little list.

The dos

1. Sit through several of the early rehearsals, even if your part isn't called, so you can suss the director out. Does she block the scene or let the actors find it? What is her terminology? Does she create a warm, creative atmosphere? What sorts of things does she say to actors? Doing this will help you understand and will prepare you for how she works with you. It also makes you aware of what you will need to do that she doesn't.
2. Do the basics. Be on time. Know your lines. Be a pleasant as well as creative part of the room. Listen carefully. Contribute. Directors notice all this. They will give more to those who are readily helpful to the process.
3. Help with the atmosphere. Some directors are better than others at creating a good working atmosphere. Be your version of friendly and polite to all. Enjoy the work of others. Actors who actually enjoy rehearsal endear themselves to directors.

4. Treat the director as a respected human, not a god or dictator. Always say hello and goodbye. Have direct eye contact. When the director says something eminently useful or insightful to you, say, "Thank you. That's great." Sympathize briefly if he has a cold. Ask her if she would like a cookie. I'm serious. Actors who don't make simple human contact scare a director. And scared directors don't give you the help you need.

5. Directors aren't always clear. (Though, of course, we think we are.) Don't be afraid to ask for clarification. "Could you help me a little more with that?" is a useful question. Always try to do what is asked of you before disagreeing. It may work better than you think. If you have questions, ask them (don't suffer in silence) but ask them nicely. It is crucial you don't create a confrontational atmosphere.

6. If you have a complex question or issue that will take some time to hash out, ask to see the director after rehearsal or before the next one. Directors would rather not bring the rehearsal to a screeching halt for an endless discussion.

7. Be specific, not general, about problems you are having with a role. Try to frame the problem so a specific answer can address it. It's better to talk about this moment or that moment rather than say general, un-addressable statements such as "I think I'm just awful in the last act." Awful how? Awful when? Directors can't fix generalities, and they know they sound silly when they try. A good way to state a problem is to propose a couple of ways of doing it and ask which is preferred.

8. If you want to try an entirely different take on a scene or moment, such as "I know we've been playing him as angry and depressed, but what if he were devastat-

ingly logical instead?" you should ask permission before changing something that has been agreed on. Say, "Is this the right moment to show you something new?" The director will tell you if it is or isn't.

9. Do compliment the director when you feel a compliment is well deserved. Even directors like intelligent compliments. We can tell, however, when you are blowing smoke. We don't like being buttered up when we know it's butter. Real interest in what's being done is always a pleasure for the director. We are in this together.

10. You can, and should, ask for more time on a moment or scene when you are sure that the time will improve the work. However, don't do this too often (unless you are playing Hamlet or Hedda), lest you be thought a rehearsal hog. Say, "Could we run those eight lines again?" or "Sometime could we have another work session on this scene?" But keep in mind that directors never have enough time. They may not be able to do what you wish immediately. The phrase "whenever you have time" helps.

And now for the don'ts

1. Discuss with the director—don't argue. The rule of thumb is that directors always win an argument, but everybody wins in a discussion.

2. Don't say that something the director proposes "won't work" or "can't be done" until you've tried it three times. Then "discuss."

3. If you are playing a smaller part and the guy playing Hamlet knows his lines before you do, the director will

notice and make negative judgments about your work habits. Remember, when you need work or want more casting, you'll wish you had been noticed positively.

4. Be very careful about what you say about a director outside rehearsal. Are there bad directors? Duh. But gossip is circular, and a surprising amount of director-bashing gets back to the director, and then you won't be happy and you'll never do another show with him. Stay out of director-bashing conversations. Really.

5. Write your blocking in your script, even if you have the proverbial elephant's memory. The director, most of the time, is creating in the moment and doesn't have it written down. Sometimes an overburdened stage manager hasn't gotten that moment down. When you haven't written it down and your memory fails and the rehearsal grinds to a halt, it is very, very embarrassing for the actor. Directors don't exactly keep score, but, if say, you're late learning your lines, you're late to rehearsals, and you don't know the blocking, the director is horrified. Your reputation is spread by the monster gossip, and your casting and career suffer.

6. Please, please, please, please do not say, "My character wouldn't do that." First, it's not "your" character; it's the playwright's character. Second, the shape of the character is a coproduction between you and the director. You don't own it. Discuss the moment but do not say... you know what.

7. Be sensible about the time you demand from the director. Everybody wants and needs her attention. When you play a small part, you get a small slice of the pie in terms of time. A middling role gets middling attention, etc. If you demand more than your share of time, the time you get is stolen from the person with three

times your stage time. Remember that there is never enough time. Have a sense of proportion. And don't keep asking, "How am I doing?" It's annoying, and it's an unanswerable question. Basically, if you are in rehearsal, you are "doing" and it's getting better. That's how you're "doing."

8. Don't give up on a note you are given because you can't accomplish it the first time. A good phrase is "I'm not getting it now, but it will be there tomorrow." Directors love actors who keep trying.

9. Don't walk into rehearsal as if the director (magical fount of all ideas) will provide all the ideas. Come in with things to try. Come in with ideas for the scene you are working on. Come in with a battle plan. Directors like actors who are co-creators. Be one.

10. If you are in the rehearsal room but not at that moment onstage, don't for heaven's sake sleep. Don't read a book or do your homework or sing show tunes. If you are in the rehearsal room, you watch the rehearsal and at least pretend to be interested. Good rehearsal room manners register with the director.

11. A final note: when you are in the professional world, you want to work with this director more than once, and when she does her first Broadway show, you want to be in the cast. When you're thirty, you'll meet people again that you worked with when you were eighteen, and they'll be directing a 140 million dollar film. You get the inference, I'm sure.

12. C'est moi! After you've gotten the part, told your friends, impressed your parents, and highlighted your lines, it's time to think about the "me, me, me." This person you are playing has an ego, a

self-image, and a way they want to be seen by others. Thinking these things over can often get you excited about playing the role.

You can only talk about these things within the context of the script. The script is your research laboratory and library. You have to be able to defend your ideas by pointing (and I mean literally pointing) to evidence in the text. "See this line and that line and the line on the next page? I think they show he's embarrassed in the company of women." If you can't find words and actions that support your thesis, abandon the thesis.

Here are twenty questions you might ask yourself after three or four readings of the complete text.

1. Would you call this character secure or insecure? Quote the text, or describe his or her actions in your answer.
2. Do you think this person has an outsized ego? An average ego? Describe a scene in the play that supports your view.
3. How would this character describe himself or herself? Can you find evidence in the text to support your view?
4. How does this character behave in the company of the other sex? Can you find a pattern in it?
5. What hurts your character's feelings and why? When her feelings are hurt, how does she behave in the script?
6. Does he have a healthy or damaged ego? Explain why.
7. How does, or would, this character describe love? Perhaps she does this very thing in the play.

8. Does this character need a little or a lot of attention? How does he go about getting it?
9. What does she think are her strengths? What does she secretly think are her weaknesses?
10. From the behavior in the text could you deduce if he thinks he is attractive? How does he use that knowledge?
11. Is there a scene in the play that inflates her ego? Is there a scene that deflates it? How does she behave when this happens?
12. When in the play does he think he is most successful and/or powerful? When does he perceive he is the weakest?
13. How would he describe what other characters think of him? In his secret heart, what does he think of himself?
14. How does she expect to be treated? How does she behave when she's not treated as she expects?
15. What are his greatest fears? Defend your idea by quoting lines or describing situations in the text.
16. Does this character think she is lovable? How can you support this view?
17. Is this character self- or other-oriented? If both, describe.
18. What makes this character angry in the play? How does this relate to his ego?
19. How does this character relate to her parents or an authority of any kind?
20. What does this character want written on his tombstone?

I often use parts of this list in discussions with the actor in rehearsal. If your director seems open to discussion you might take up one or two of these questions with her—the answer might set off an interesting and lively exchange of ideas.

Remember, your character's behavior and emotional landscape are most often defined by their expectations and those expectations are most often formed by self-image. To get a sense of this self-image, do an improv where you (as the character) try to define yourself to a dating service, to a possible employer, and to a parole board. You'll be surprised by the positive acting ideas this generates.

One more thing: a great secret in acting is simply *variety*. How we feel about ourselves is obviously situational. In high school, I felt one way about myself onstage, another way on the basketball court, another way with my parents, and yet another way on a date. In each case my ego functioned differently. It even functioned differently at various places on the basketball court.

Track your character's ego and self-image throughout the play. Scene one: She's at work, new on the job, inexperienced, and her self-image is a roller coaster. She's on top of the situation with the guy who flirts with her at the water cooler, but when her manager walks up she disappears into the woodwork. Scene two: At her father's bedside in the hospital. She feels helpless. She drops things. She knows he's always felt she was a klutz and that makes her become one. If you asked her her height, she would say, "two foot eight." Scene three: At the taekwondo completion. She's a champion. She greets people with complete ease and confidence. For the first time we see that she's funny!

Ego and self-image don't flatten your performance. In point of fact, they give the peaks and valleys that make a great performance. The ego at work often gives us new insight and new possibilities.

Let's say our character is known for her fashion sense

but discovers her new Jason Wu gown has a horrible stain in the back from sitting on a shrimp and avocado hors d'oeuvre. Horrors, people will laugh! So instead of displaying her usual gracious manner, she is unpleasant and short with people. Her ego and self-image is under fire, whether anybody else thinks so or not. It's the "me, me, me" at work.

In the next scene she's back to being generally admired and is pleasant as pie. It's all one character, right? But from scene to scene, her self-image produces different characteristics, and that makes her more interesting to an audience.

The action, what your character wants, is always key. But the "me, me, me" flavors the action differently from moment to moment. And therein, my acting friends, lies a useful acting tool.

6. C'est moi!

After you've gotten the part, told your friends, impressed your parents, and highlighted your lines, it's time to think about the "me, me, me." This person you are playing has an ego, a self-image, and a way they want to be seen by others. Thinking these things over can often get you excited about playing the role.

You can only talk about these things within the context of the script The script is your research laboratory and library. You have to be able to defend your ideas by pointing (and I mean literally pointing) to evidence in the text "See this line and that line and the line on the next page? I think they show he's embarrassed in the company of women." If you can't find words and actions that support your thesis, abandon the thesis.

Here are twenty questions you might ask yourself after three or four readings of the complete text.

1. Would you call this character secure or insecure? Quote the text, or describe his or her actions in your answer.
2. Do you think this person has an outsized ego? An average ego? Describe a scene in the play that supports your view.
3. How would this character describe himself or herself? Can you find evidence in the text to support your view?
4. How does this character behave in the company of

the other sex? Can you find a pattern in it?
5. What hurts your character's feelings and why? When her feelings are hurt, how does she behave in the script?
6. Does he have a healthy or damaged ego? Explain why.
7. How does, or would, this character describe love? Perhaps she does this very thing in the play.
8. Does this character need a little or a lot of attention? How does he go about getting it?
9. What does she think are her strengths? What does she secretly think are her weaknesses?
10. From the behavior in the text could you deduce if he thinks he is attractive? How does he use that knowledge?
11. Is there a scene in the play that inflates her ego? Is there a scene that deflates it? How does she behave when this happens?
12. When in the play does he think he is most successful and/or powerful? When does he perceive he is the weakest?
13. How would he describe what other characters think of him? In his secret heart, what does he think of himself?
14. How does she expect to be treated? How does she behave when she's not treated as she expects?
15. What are his greatest fears? Defend your idea by quoting lines or describing situations in the text.
16. Does this character think she is lovable? How can you support this view?
17. Is this character self- or other-oriented? If both, describe.
18. What makes this character angry in the play? How does this relate to his ego?

19. How does this character relate to her parents or an authority of any kind?
20. What does this character want written on his tombstone?

I often use parts of this list in discussions with the actor in rehearsal. If your director seems open to discussion you might take up one or two of these questions with her—the answer might set off an interesting and lively exchange of ideas.

Remember, your character's behavior and emotional landscape are most often defined by their expectations and those expectations are most often formed by self-image. To get a sense of this self-image, do an improv where you (as the character) try to define yourself to a dating service, to a possible employer, and to a parole board. You'll be surprised by the positive acting ideas this generates.

One more thing: a great secret in acting is simply variety. How we feel about ourselves is obviously situational. In high school, I felt one way about myself onstage, another way on the basketball court, another way with my parents, and yet another way on a date. In each case my ego functioned differently. it even functioned differently at various places on the basketball court.

Track your character's ego and self-image throughout the play. Scene one: She's at work, new on the job, inexperienced, and her self-image is a roller coaster. She's on top of the situation with the guy who flirts with her at the water cooler, but when her manager walks up she disappears into the woodwork Scene two: At her father's bedside in the hospital. She feels helpless. She drops things. She knows he's always felt she was a klutz and that makes her become one. If you asked her her height, she would say, "two foot eight." Scene three: At the taekwondo completion. She's a champion. She greets people with complete ease and confidence.

For the first time we see that she's funny!

Ego and self-image don't flatten your performance. In point of fact, they give the peaks and valleys that make a great performance. The ego at work often gives us new insight and new possibilities.

Let's say our character is known for her fashion sense but discovers her new Jason Wu gown has a horrible stain in the back from sitting on a shrimp and avocado hors d'oeuvre. Horrors, people will laugh! So instead of displaying her usual gracious manner, she is unpleasant and short with people. Her ego and self-image is under fire, whether anybody else thinks so or not. It's the "me, me, me" at work.

In the next scene she's back to being generally admired and is pleasant as pie. It's all one character, right? But from scene to scene, her self-image produces different characteristics, and that makes her more interesting to an audience.

The action, what your character wants, is always key. But the "me, me, me" flavors the action differently from moment to moment. And therein, my acting friends, lies a useful acting tool.

7. Acting problem number one

Okay, here's a genuine difficulty: you're concentrating, you're using the given circumstances, the emotion is boiling up in you, you're energized, you're hot as a pistol. You are feeling it, baby!

And it all sounds the same.

This is "acting problem number one," and what is scary is that acting theory—be it Stanislavski, Stella Adler, Sanford Meisner, or the opinions of your Aunt Harriet, who once appeared in *No, No, Nanette*—doesn't confront this problem directly. The general idea is that if you are fully in the situation, have a backstory, believe what you are doing, and are pursuing the objective, it won't all sound the same. Well, it ain't necessarily so.

I have taught thousands of acting classes, and the majority of the work I see and hear there tends to be musically on one note and rhythmically steady as a metronome and thus creates what steady repetition has always produced... boredom. Boredom, may we agree, isn't the best possible end result of acting, right?

What is difficult and even depressing is that this boring acting is often honest and believable, which we know is a good acting result. Confusing, no? If honest and believable ain't got rhythm, what we got is an acting problem. Just because something is true and lifelike doesn't mean it's interesting, holds attention, and keeps the audience from going back to reading their programs.

Now, in a certain sense, the solution is simple. The problem is solved by this true, lifelike, honest, and believable acting also containing the following elements: loud and soft, fast and slow, and God willing, syncopation. Syncopation is that which displaces the beats or accents, so that strong beats become weak and vice versa. In speech, it might mean dropping sounds or letters in the middle of the word. Anyway, syncopation is a kind of advanced form of variety. So let's, for the moment, just stick with loud and soft, fast and slow, and short and long groupings of words.

Warning on the bottle: this kind of variety, unless backed up by belief and intent, makes for terrible acting. On the other hand, there is no good acting that doesn't contain those elements.

Let's work on a short speech: "Look, I don't want to talk about this. As a matter of fact, I don't want to talk to you, period. Sit there, kick off your shoes, drink a 7-Up, watch *Breaking Bad* reruns, and most importantly, do not say a single word! Silence is what I want to hear." Say it once. Believe it. Good.

Now let's mess with the above elements. To do so we need to talk about the "run-on sentence." This simply means pay no attention to the punctuation—in this case, the periods. Take these two sentences, "Look, I don't want to talk about this. As a matter of fact I don't want to talk to you, period." To make it a run-on, you simply remove the period and say both sentences without a break, as if they were one sentence. Try it. Good.

Using run-on sentences from time to time breaks up the speech rhythmically. There are only four sentences. Try this in the speech: say the first two sentences as a run-on and the last two sentences as a run-on. Now say the speech that way. Good.

Now say the first sentence alone and the last three sentences as a ran-on. Good. Now say the first three sentences as a run-on and the last sentence after a pause. Good. Now say the first sentence, take a pause. Say the second sentence, take a pause. Now say the last two sentences as a run-on. Good. This creates meaning through rhythm, right?

Now using the same speech, let's mess with fast and slow. Say the first sentence slowly. Say the second sentence slowly. Wait. That wasn't slow enough. Do it again. Now say the third sentence as quickly as possible while maintaining sense. Not quick enough. Do it again. Now say the last sentence very slowly. Now put the whole speech together using those instructions. Good.

Okay, it's time for those old favorites: loud and soft. Say the first two sentences as a run-on but very softly. Say the third sentence loudly. Say the fourth sentence softly. No, softer than that. As a matter of fact, whisper that last sentence. Good. Now do the whole speech again that way but make the phrase "Do not say a single word" way louder than anything in the speech. Good.

Let's do it again but follow these instructions. One sentence must be very loud, one very soft, one very fast, and one very slow. You pick which ones. Do it again. Keep that structure but strive to make the work believable. Do it once more. Good.

All right, it's time for your graduation. Do the speech so it includes fast, slow, louder, softer, and a run-on sentence. Do it. Good. Do it again. Good. Do it once more, striving to make it honest and believable.

This is a short workout with elements of variety that are crucial to acting. The goal is to work with these elements long enough that you don't have to think about them, they are just there. In the beginning, they will conflict with your instincts, but eventually the use of these elements will *become* instinctual.

Athletes are experts at turning techniques into instinctual behavior. They work on the mechanics over and over and over, until their use becomes natural. Actors often turn away from technique because it makes it hard to "get out of my head." Of course it does, but that feeling is a pass-through on the way to better and more interesting work.

The exercises we have done are the most obvious and simplest of ways to create rhythm and variety. There are worlds of others, but if I'm not mistaken, we need to start somewhere on the road to playing jazz Actors are jazz musicians of the text, and someday, further down the road, you'll hear the greatest compliment: "That cat can really blow."

8. The back and forth

Why, why, why is it so hard for actors to react? I've been teaching college undergraduates and grad students for fifteen years, and the ability to react to what other actors are doing is where the rubber meets the road... and far too often doesn't.

So here's the deal: first you have to have an objective—something you want. If you don't, then you aren't acting, you're just displaying, or to be brutal, just showing off. Now, your character wants something and the other character (all gods willing) reacts to how you are going about getting it. Huzzah! We are now two-thirds of the way to something we could describe as "acting."

This is also the moment when your work can turn to dog doo. You now have to revise what you are doing based on the other character's reaction. Crash, splinter, tinkle.... the scene falls apart. If Actor A—that's you—doesn't react to Actor B's reaction, we're off the rails, lost in the underbrush of C-minus acting. Why, why, why? Well, I can list some reasons:

1. You've planned what you are going to do and you are going to do that come hell or high water. Your planning gives you a sense of control, but that iron control also makes your acting suck. Did I just say your acting sucks? How rude. But it does.

   Why do actors choose this iron control? Maybe because it's a way of keeping the unknown at bay. By doing all the things you have planned, in the order you planned to do them, you're able to suppress "acting fear," our greatest enemy. But that kind of controlled performance also suppresses creativity, which is... well... a very bad thing. It sort of turns the scene into an acting graveyard where only the ghosts of actual acting come out to play at curtain time.

Let's think about this for a minute. Doing what you have planned to do independent of what the other person does would make you a terrible, ghastly, no-good ping-pong player. It would make you a reviled lover. It would make you an endlessly defeated general. That's enough examples. Let's just return to the idea that it will make your acting suck.

2. Another reason some actors don't react to other actors is that they are basically nonreactors in life. Sad as it is, and as long as they continue to do what they do independent of what you do, they should stay away from acting and become horrible bosses, which is often what happens.

3. It might be that you don't react spontaneously to what the other actor does because you are frightened (scared, spooked, immobilized), and in this state you really can't do much of anything, let alone act. I like number three—I can work with that. Everybody's scared but if you keep on keeping on, that fear will reduce and become so small, so unimportant that it will get out of your way and let you react. Just give yourself some time, unless.

4. Unless nobody ever told you that reacting readily to what other people say and do is the gold standard of acting. Well, now somebody has told you.

What are these reactions we are talking about? Physical reactions, big and small. These are what is popularly called *body language*. A physical reaction may have to do with space, as in "what you just said is so upsetting to me that I have to move away from you, or I go into a protective shell by crossing my legs and arms." Or it may be that your expression changes from a smile to a frown. Or it may be a dismissive gesture or the positive reinforcement of a hug. Or you may freeze with a bottle of water halfway to your lips.

It may be a new thought or change of thoughts regarding the way you achieve your objective, as in: "Wow, she's really hostile. How should I handle that?" This reaction may be only visible in your eyes or it may cause you to throw back your head and stare at the ceiling. Or what she does may make you freeze and do nothing so she won't know what you're thinking.

The reaction could be verbal, in terms of how you say your next line in response to her. The line "I love you" can be warm and demonstrative or cold and threatening, making it clear your love is conditional. It can also be tone of voice that gives the impression of your reaction.

All the while you are recalibrating the ways you can achieve your objective, as in, "Flirting with her isn't working in trying to borrow her car. I need to be firmer about the fact she owes me."

Sometimes the reaction is instinctive, as in, "She's about to spill her coffee on my computer," and almost without thinking you pull it away.

Now this goes on and on for the length of play. It's not one moment, it's a thousand moments. You do something, she does something in response, you do something because of her response, she does something because your response, etc., etc., etc.

It takes concentration. You must concentrate on getting what you want and then make course corrections based on what she is saying and doing until you get it. The objective is firm. The tactics to achieve what you want are ever-changing until you achieve it. Once an action is achieved (she let me borrow her car!), a new objective begins (will you come with me? I'm scared) and reactions begin afresh. You have to trust yourself in the same way a juggler does in keeping five balls in the air. Unfortunately this chain of reaction isn't negotiable: you have to do it.

That is, of course, unless you don't mind if you suck. And I know you do mind, so play a little ping-pong and stop trying to control everything you do.

9. Between the lines

So you say something, and then I say something, and after a couple of hours, that's a play. What is a good deal of fun is thinking about what happens after you say something to me.

Florida
  A play

Robert: I don't care what you say. We've got the tickets, and we're going to Florida.

Lynette: You can take Florida and stuff it up your nose.

(Lights out.)
End of play.

Now, what happens between Robert saying "We're going to Florida" and Lynette saying "You can take Florida and stuff it" is fascinating.

Here are some options:

1. As soon as Lynette hears him say the word "tickets," she knows he's talking about Florida. She has heard about the cases of Zika virus there and is definitely, 100 percent, not going, no way, forget it! Thus, even before

he says the words "to Florida," she starts her line, you can take Florida..." Thus, for a couple of words they are both talking. This is called *jumping the cue.*

2. She pretty much knows what he is going to say, but her grandmother has taught her not to interrupt while someone is speaking, so when she hears his last word, "Florida," she starts her line when she hears the "d" in "Florida." This is called *tight cuing.*

3. Lynette doesn't want to go to Florida, but she thinks it's nice he wants to be with her so, very calmly and with a radiant smile, she starts her line less than a second after he has said the word "Florida." This is called *picking up the cue.*

4. She is not completely sure about her position on the Florida question, and when Robert forcefully says, "We're going to Florida," she needs to think. This means there is a clear, maybe even significant, pause after Robert says the word "Florida" before she speaks. That pause, depending on her thought process and emotional state, could last two to ten seconds. This is called *laying off the cue.*

Let's recap:

1. Starting your line before his line is finished: jumping the cue

2. Speaking off the final consonant of his last word: tight cuing

3. Speaking just after he has definitely finished: picking up the cue

4. Waiting a bit after the end of his line while you think before speaking: laying off the cue

The secret is to mix up these four kinds of working with the cue to provide a sensible variety and rhythm that reflect your mental state throughout the play.

Say he has four lines, thus providing you with four cues. You now have options—many, many options. You could tight cue the first three and lay off the fourth. You could pick up the first two normally and then jump the third and tight cue the fourth. You have so many options it would take a passionate mathematician to figure out how many combinations are possible with just four cues.

Hold on, I'll give you an eight-line exercise you can spend a half hour on with your friendly neighborhood theatre nerd.

No. 1: Hey, okay, but I think you're all talk and no action.

No. 2: Can we just let this drop?

No. 1: You said you'd like to fill his car with cement.

No. 2: Kidding.

No. 1: Let's do it; you can rent cement mixers.

No. 2: It's like three a.m., and your mind has turned to limeade.

No. 1: I am, cross my heart, deadly, completely, wholeheartedly serious.

No. 2: Fine. Get us a mixer.

Both people in the scene have the four options on each cue. Run it five or six times and change your choices each time. Why are we even talking about this? Because variety is crucial to a good performance. Whenever the audience knows not only what is coming next, but also how it will be coming, they check out and start thinking whether they should get hair extensions. The only rule that cannot be broken in acting is: Don't do the same thing all the time.

The good news about mixing up your cuing is that with a little practice, it becomes spontaneous. You don't have to sit in your parked car in the Walmart parking lot and plan what you're going to do. This isn't an artificial rhythm; it devolves from character, plot, and the psychology of the moment. Learning acting is really just a process of understanding the options open to you and then picking one. Acting and life are the process of making choices. Actors continually make choices in the pursuit of the objective and the obstacles to attaining the objective, right? You now have choices about handling the cue. Use 'em or lose 'em.

10. The walking dead

What a joy it is to play a big, fat scene with a responsive, talented, prepared, energetic scene mate. And then there's the opposite scenario: there you are in the scene you've been waiting for all year, and you're playing with a semi-comatose, dead-on-their-feet, obviously unprepared, blank-eyed piece of living statuary who is obviously vice president of the Walking Dead Society. You could cheerfully pinch him until he was black and blue or avoid the whole thing by going to law school.

What now, oh thespian? Well, here's a thought or two.

Sometimes you can wake the zombie-actor by touching him. Touch is a powerful weapon in the acting arsenal. If I didn't work to convince the actors in my class that touching the other actor is neither illegal nor fattening, we might go a whole semester without anybody touching anybody. Why? Well, it's societal, for a start. Italians and Bulgarians touch each other as a matter of course. Obviously, we're talking about touch without sexual overtones or intent. Americans, on the other hand—puritans that we are—seem to feel that touch is dangerous, misleading, and something of a car bomb. By touching the zombie-actor's shoulder, or giving them a discreet pat or a whack on the back, you can suddenly wake them. They may even go so far as to react to you.

Touch often frees an actor, sort of like Sleeping Beauty waking up after a kiss. Try it. Or, get really close—within two feet. In life, people hold most conversations no more than three to four feet apart. On stage they chat away at field-goal distance. Why? Because that's where the director put them. Why? Don't ask. Anyway, move in close and speak louder than usual. This will surprise the zombie and usually wake him up for a while, so some actual acting can go on.

How do you identify actual acting? People are reacting to each other, that's how. You know it, I know it—only the zombie doesn't. You will notice that in all my suggestions there is an element of change, surprise, or demand, something that reminds the zombie that he's alive, something that catches him unprepared. The secret is to break out of the formal structure into the spontaneous, provoking reaction by surprise. My hope is that the zombie will enjoy it. Often he does.

I just mentioned the word "demand." The dictionary (the world's best acting book) calls it an "insistent and preemptory request." Something in our acting must demand, in no uncertain terms, that the zombie awake. The problem may be that on that particular day you are part zombie yourself. Horrors! Two zombies playing a scene? The audience could either run or, more likely, sleep. Non-zombie actors must demand, require, insist, berate—something! Here is where "I want" turns into "I must." Make the zombie do something. This is the best zombie medicine we have.

Of course, it's possible he's not a zombie but just afraid—shy of acting, shy of making a mistake, plain old afraid. Befriend the zombie (or in this case, the pseudo-zombie). Actors who are afraid—and we all are at some point—need your simple humanity. You know how to offer friendship, right? Do that. Say hello and make a little small talk before rehearsal starts. Find something to compliment in their acting. Bring cookies. Tell a joke. Actor fear responds well to kindness. And once the other person trusts you a little and has been treated warmly and with respect, you may not need the other antidotes we've discussed.

The reactive actor makes the other actor active. Fifty percent of acting is reacting. Hone your reactive skills, and it empowers the other actor to do the same. And, dear teachers and directors, insist that your charges become more reactive. Often, they don't even realize they are zombies. Do reaction drills. Give reaction notes. Praise reactivity. Doing too much reacting at a certain stage of development is a positive. I'm talking about visible reaction, not deeply buried internal reaction. We need to see acting as well as feel acting.

Help a zombie today. Otherwise, the zombie will eat your energy and interest and leave your performance vague, uninspiring, and as wilted as week-old lettuce. Don't accept the zombie scene. Say that three times today before you go into rehearsal.

11 Things people do

Here are four things people do that actors don't do enough.

1. Lose

In life we lose all the time. You take something back to the store and all they'll give you is store credit, and you hate the store. Your argument in favor of ending the death penalty fails to persuade anyone in your civics class. You're caught using the same knife you just used to scoop butter into your baked potato to scoop more butter. We lose small battles all day long.

Now why don't we see more of that in your acting? I sometimes think people go into acting to inhabit a world where they lose less often. I am here to tell you that losing is one of the richest sources of good acting. Make losing an integral part of your work.

An example:

Losing actor: I have no idea where your scissors went.

Winning actor: I just found them on your desk.

You just lost. *Act* that. You could slap your forehead, laugh humorlessly, sulk, obviously change the subject, pretend you didn't hear, narrow your eyes in annoyance, sit down disconsolately, or a hundred other things. Make the loss part of the next moment you play.

Yes, sometimes the losing is made overt in the next line you say, but many times it isn't. To lose convincingly you need to know what your character wanted and didn't get. So like most things in acting, you can't lose unless you wanted something. In the above example about double-dipping the butter, you might lose because you were right in the middle of trying to impress the other person. Maybe it's your first meal with your boyfriend's or girlfriend's parents.

Actors who neglect to lose on stage usually aren't clear about what they wanted in the first place. Here's a practice drill: go back and read the script you're working on to identify a dozen places where your character "loses," and then make sure of your character's response. Don't just ride on by.

2. Let your characters be critical of what they say

How many times do we devoutly wish we could walk the words we have said back into our mouth? Many, right? We don't like the way we said it. We don't like when we said it. We wish we hadn't said it. It wasn't polite to say it. We realize we're repeating ourselves, etc., etc., etc. I think character self-criticism is underused because we didn't say it, the playwright did—and playwrights always say what they mean, right? Well, if our characters are going to be lifelike, they have to be fallible, and some of what's said in plays is definitely fallible.

An example:

Your character: You look beautiful tonight.
You just screwed up. You implied she didn't look beau-

tiful this afternoon, and she hasn't changed. Why didn't you say, "You look as beautiful as ever," or why didn't you just shut up and kiss her? Why, why are you so clumsy? Now there's an acting moment, so act it.

Another example:

Your character: Please, please stop yelling!

You just screwed up. He wasn't actually yelling, it was just... forceful. If you'd shut up, it would have blown over in a minute, but no, you had to provoke an all-out fight. Take the moment to act that. Look through the script for the opportunities to develop this sense of self-criticism in your character. She may be our heroine, but she doesn't know that. Words, in our own lives, are almost the hardest thing to get right... right?

3. Let your character agree or disagree with people *while* they are talking

This is simple, but try it. The overarching idea is that, as the character, we are either agreeing or disagreeing internally with everything that is said to us. Maybe not every word, but certainly every complete thought we hear. So, react visibly: slightly nod your head "yes" when you agree, slightly shake your head "no" when you disagree, and don't do a thing when you aren't sure.

Why? Well, obviously, it forces your beleaguered brain to pay attention. It builds concentration and critical faculty, and it makes thought process visible. Despite the fact you are thinking complex, utterly fascinating, and germane thoughts, I may not be able to read those thoughts from my seat in Row S, but hey, I'm really interested.

Now this acting tip is basically for rehearsal, but you might want to retain some of this head-work in performance. Thought made visible is an acting necessity, whether you are on stage or in front of the camera.

4. Talk to yourself

To finish up so that you can stop reading and start doing, let's talk about talking. Some of the time we're talking to the other person and sometimes we're talking to ourselves.

An example:

Your character: Hey, do you have any tea, any herbal tea? I'm feeling... not nauseous but more... I don't know, I'm out of it.

Now in the first sentence you are obviously talking to the other person, and in the second you are using words to inquire of yourself. In life we do this constantly. Listen to the people around you and place what they say into these two categories. It's as if at one moment we pursue an objective to get the other person to do our will and the next we are trying to define something for ourselves.

Oddly, on stage, this distinction often gets lost. I see pieces of work every day where all the talking seems directed outward, which, begging your pardon, isn't, well... lifelike. A simple distinction might be that when speaking to others we seek some response, while in speaking to ourselves it is more reflective and your answer to what you have asked yourself may remain unspoken.

The point is to get these different usages of language more clearly into your acting. Try taking an audition piece and dividing it into the two categories. Now act it that way. Sounds different now, right?

Jon Jory

In acting, not every character you play strives to be lifelike. Sometimes you're a metaphor, a symbol, or an imaginary alien from planet X34. But let's be real (literally): in the overwhelming majority of cases, you want to get the audience to relate to you by showing them a set of recognizable behaviors. E.T. looked funny, but he wanted to "go home."

We've talked about four ways to build this recognition. That way, when I see you on stage, I'll find your acting more... well... human.

12. Taking stage

Stop feeling bad about being a bit of an acting piggy. Wanting the focus, wanting the audience attention, and doing a little "Me, me, me!" isn't as horrible as we're told—when it serves the play. Back in the old days, when actors wore grease paint (horrible, slimy stuff that gets all over your costume) acting this way was simply called "taking stage." It meant that the audience, fickle creatures that they are, should be looking at and listening to you and not to Emily at that point in the script, even though Emily was wearing a dress made of reflective silver sequins and had glorious, curly blonde hair down to her waist. So, making sure the focus was where it should be was called "taking stage," and sitting quietly, not moving or gesturing while looking at the actor who was giving his big speech about how he became a serial killer, was called "giving stage."

I was thinking about this the other day in class when two actors were doing the devastating final scene in Neil LaBute's *The Shape of Things,* where the young man named Adam discovers that his torrid romance with an art student whom he wishes to marry was, in reality, her thesis project for her M.F.A. without any emotional involvement on her part. She has invited him to the opening of her art show, where he discovers that recordings of their lovemaking, his letters and clothes, etc. are part of the installation.

The scene is tense, angry, and despairing with emotional pain, and public humiliation is passed around like cookies. The actress gave a highly intelligent, controlled performance—still and icy—but the problem was that I had spent 90 percent of the time looking and listening to the other actor. He commanded the scene vocally and physically in terms of the flux and flow of his feelings and attacks. He simultaneously walked away with the scene and destroyed it. So, how do you demand attention for your half of the scene so the play will work?

First, you can't allow the other actor to continually dominate you vocally. If his vocal attack is steadily louder and more energetic, you and your voice are likely to be lost in the shuffle. You must, at least in key moments, match him vocally. A sharp attack vocally at the beginning of each sentence can even things out. If he shouts, you can even the scene by taking a substantial (two- or three-beat) pause after he finishes. The audience will now be ready to listen to you when you speak. If your voice and the use of it don't command attention, the audience won't understand what's happening in the scene.

Actors with a larger gestural vocabulary than you, and whose bodies are more responsive to the words they speak, get the most attention. Sometimes too darned much, if the scene partner draws no visual interest. Yes, stillness can draw the eye, but it may not retain the eye if stillness is all there is. In *The Shape of Things* scene, the actress' continual stillness became way too much of a good thing. What her partner was doing with greater physical openness helped the audience understand the lines. The physicality was also the language of his emotions. The actor needs to mix stillness and physicality, otherwise the audience keeps hoping for the opposite of what you're doing. Thus, you might move from stillness to physicality at a key moment in the scene or, of course, the opposite. If you're sitting and you want a line to land, change the way you are sitting in the chair as you say it. The physical move attracts our attention and the line secures it. You are taking stage.

Thinking is another way of taking stage. Let's say your speech has five sentences, and the third, "So, I'm not staying here another day," is the emotional center of the speech. Play the first three sentences quickly and take a pause, formulating the perfect words for the third sentence before speaking it. Then take another pause to think about what you've said. Then say the last two sentences quickly, almost offhandedly. Your thoughts frame the crucial sentence and make it take stage.

Obviously, taking stage with your voice, body, or mind demands your knowledge of the moments in the scene that define, heighten, and reveal it. Yes, taking stage is a crucial skill for the actor, but, more important, when do you do it? Scene analysis by the actor and director helps decide the most important moments for character and story. Then your skill at taking stage enlightens rather than simply gains attention. The actor must not simply assume the audience's attention but demand it. Do you do that?

13. The right touch

I once kept track during a set of scenes done for an acting class final, and in the eight scenes, no actor ever touched another actor. No touch of any kind, not even with a fingertip.

Hmmm... Why?

I think because in American culture, touch is considered rude and even explosive outside the handshake and, in the theatre world, the hug. How wonderful for the actor! Anything proscribed or overlooked in real life becomes instantly theatrical onstage. Breaking a taboo wakes everybody up, and that includes our friends in the audience. Sex in all its forms has become commonplace in film and television, while remaining less ordinary onstage. Strangely, a film may contain the steamiest moments of human sexuality and once that's over, there may be no other example of touch in the movie.

Except, of course, violence. Apparently, it's fine to make love to someone or kill them as long as you never touch them in any other circumstance. How deliciously odd!

What I am circling around here are the uses that other forms of touch have for the actor.

1. Touch as a wake-up call. Actors have often sought me out privately to complain in repressed but outraged tones that some other actor "isn't giving me anything." Well, one explanation for this is that the actors in this state of non-giving are so deep in their own heads and

processes that, practically speaking, other actors onstage have effectively ceased to exist for them. They aren't giving you anything because you only tangentially are there.

So here's what to do: touch them. Your touch will wake them just like the prince's kiss woke Sleeping Beauty. No, I'm not suggesting you walk over and kiss them, or kill them. Reach over and touch them with a fingertip on their arm as you begin your speech. Brush a crumb off their jacket, a fly off their arm. A quick, reassuring pat, say. You will be amazed to find that for the first time in Act Two, they actually play the next moments with you. You will have called them forth from the cave of their self-concern. Try it; it's quite magical.

2. Touch as a demand. There are always certain moments in any play you perform where your character has something to say that he desperately wants heard. This line, in terms of plot and character, is crucial. This line is a big moment and moves the story forward—it changes everything, and the audience needs to know that.

Break social convention and expectation by *demanding* through touch. Turn the other person firmly to face you. Or, say, stop her from going where she is headed. Or, give her a little hit that shocks but doesn't harm. Allow whatever touch you use to be insistent and surprising, but not violent. The audience fully understands that the social conventions that lead us not to touch have been broken and that they better listen up. This is touch as dramaturgy as well as psychology. Find that crucial moment in the play where a touch insists on being heard and understood.

3. Touch also creates wonderful moments when you withdraw. You empathetically put your hand on your sis-

ter's shoulder the moment before you tell her that her husband has been unfaithful. The next big moment will be when you withdraw your hand—when the hand disappears and something colder, even judgmental, enters the room. Touch can wake a big moment, and the withdrawal of touch wakes another.

Don't waste touch. Make the end of touching another emotional state.

By touching, you also give the other actor a chance to make a point by terminating the touch. You touch them to assure them of your affection or caring. They create conflict by removing themselves from your touch. Your touch can set off a cascade of meaning and deepening of relationship or conflict.

4. All right, I know, we need to talk about touch in terms of romance or simply getting it on. The first time touch occurs is a big moment. What is the first moment Juliet touches Romeo, or the other way around? You're going to want to think that over. Too early, and he seems seductive and practiced rather than enthralled. Too late, and the sexual tension will have evaporated.

  In romance, touch is earned. What's the right moment to touch Romeo? That touch commits you. When is it right to be committed? If you make touch commonplace, you make the relationship commonplace. On the other hand, that might be what's needed. Remember the saying "timing is everything"? Take that into account.

5. What kind of touch when? Touch is, obviously, visible psychology. If you are, as I hope, a devotee of the objective (what do you want?), then touch becomes another

arrow in your quiver. If touching another human being is a special moment, then touch and "need" are almost Siamese twins. When the "need" gets strong enough, we break through the social rules, spoken or unspoken, against touch and everyone in the room realizes something special and important has happened.

Your need would have to be great, for instance, to touch your boss. What about someone you've just met? If you don't want someone to think you are romantically interested in her, then you would only touch her out of some other profound need.

Touch has its own vocabulary. Flirting is one sort of touch, warning another. Just let touch respond to the moment. The point is to make touch a greater part of our acting vocabulary.

We should speak for a moment about how touch works in rehearsal. You obviously don't just walk up to another actor and slap <u>him</u> or smooch him without warning. Extreme forms of touch need discussion and agreement before being employed. On the other hand, if you have the impulse to place a warning finger on another character's chest, you need to be able to do so. Most touch can be spontaneous and then discussed if it seems in some sense wrong.

Acting is an unusual profession. You meet people for the first time at a reading, and two days later, you are fighting them to the death with actual swords and daggers, or ripping off their clothes. The point here is that the touch you employ reflects the script's relationship and not how long you've been rehearsing. How you touch defines that particular character and that particular situation at that particular moment. Loosen up. Touch somebody. It's too useful a tool to be shy about.

14. Moving parts

Stage movement. Oh my. There are so many styles, philosophies, systems, and adherents that there is really no way to get hold of it in an article. But we're in the theatre, right? Using words to describe the impossible is our wheelhouse. Sooooo let me set part of what could be talked about outside the fence and then deal with what's left inside.

I'm not going to talk about the myriad forms of dance, nor Viewpoints, nor Suzuki, nor mask work, nor commedia, nor clowning. I will touch on these estimable systems and pleasures as preparation for the body to do ordinary stage movement in an ordinary play with ordinary dialogue—or as we like to say, realism.

Most actors most of the time are going to be earning their daily bread moving around in kitchens, living rooms, parking garages, and backyards. How do you teach the actor those physicalities? The answer is we teach them Viewpoints, Suzuki, clown work, etc. The next question is, do these disciplines open up and improve the actor in their daily grind of realism? My answer is unfortunately, nuh-uh.

The people who pursue these movement disciplines will vehemently disagree, but as a director who has worked in excellent professional settings on semi and full-out realistic plays, I'm not convinced. These actors come into my rehearsal directly out of a two-hour clowning class and stand around in the play like sticks and statues, giving the distinct impression they have no idea what to do with this body they must cart around.

Why? Because of the addition of text and the necessities of story, that's why. You can argue with me until your last breath that your Suzuki class has improved your physical work in Miller's *Death of a Salesman,* and I will tell you I can't see it. Movement work has improved your body and your stamina, which is preparation but not the actual physicality open to you while you sit on a bunkbed and talk to your brother Biff. For that we need to create a new class in the curriculum called "The Complexity of Realistic Movement." Are they teaching that in your acting program?

Movement in a realistic play comes from three sources—emotion, task, and objective. Emotion: you hear Jimmy has stolen your car and in frustration you turn in a tight circle and throw punches at the air. Task: Betty comes over to tell you her sister doesn't find you attractive, but you decide to offer her a cup of coffee, and fixing the coffee has its own physicality. Objective: you want Arturo to leave because he is drunk and disorderly, so you take his arm, pull him out of the chair, and push him over to the door.

Actually there's a fourth source (though it's related to emotion), and that's the physicality generated by saying words, given what you feel about those words. This last is key in producing gesture, and gesture is a gigantic vocabulary within which most actors work with severe limitations. Most people's gestural vocabulary sucks and doesn't change enormously no matter what character or in what situation they find themselves. Many actors have a gestural vocabulary so limited that we might say it operates at a fourth-grade level. So, curriculum nerds, acting programs need to insert a course in gestural vocabulary generally. The advanced course would be in developing character through gestural vocabulary suitable to realism. This would help the actor get and nail the two hundred jobs that will represent a career. The clowning class will help with three jobs. Hmmm, which should be in the curriculum?

What, you might ask, are some of the things that would happen in these classes? Here is a tasting menu:

1. Most young actors I work with tend to gesture narrowly and from, at best, the elbow. They need to practice getting their hands away from their bodies while speaking. Design your own exercise that includes making sense of a realistic speech while at one point getting your hands over your head.
2. There are staccato gestures and round gestures. Young actors tend to prefer the staccato, as in jabbing or poking, to the round gestures based on all or part of a circle. Your gestural vocabulary needs both. Do a six- or eight-line scene with another person where they do staccato and you do round. Make us believe you. Now reverse.
3. Most young actors start a gesture from the hip, where their hands are hanging, and after the gesture their hands, exhausted, fall back to their original position at the hip. I call this "gunfighter" acting. Do an exercise (always with dialogue) in which wherever your hands travel to in a gesture, you keep them there instead of letting them fall back limply to your hip. Then start a second gesture, and when that gesture is complete, keep your hands at the end point for a sentence or two and then allow a third gesture. Do this while acting "to be or not to be."
4. The whole position a body takes at rest is actually a form of gesture as well as architecture. Sit in a chair nine different ways. Very good. Now do nine more. While talking.

5. Do a monologue sitting on a sofa. During the speech, change your position on the sofa five times. Make me believe the speech.

Halftime.

There are two different sorts of gesture, the first being "intuitive." This is when what you are talking about jacks your body around (including your hands) to punctuate or orchestrate the words and your feelings about them. The second category is "intentional." This is when you point which way to go while giving directions, etc., or say, you clap your hands to make a bobcat go away.

6. While doing a scene, allow both intuitive and intentional gesture. Use quite a bit, just for giggles. Make me believe your work.
7. Write a piece of material where each of two characters has only one speech and each speech has six sentences. Give each actor three moderately odd gestures (such as hitting their forehead twice with a closed fist or poking one finger four times into the other open palm) Then do the scene. Make us believe it.
8. Do this same scene again with each actor gesturing three times with their feet. Gesture is not just a province of the hands and arms.

Enough.

The point of this Realistic Movement class is to include the body, arms, and legs in an expansion of the actor's gestural vocabulary in a way that enhances the meaning and emotion of the realistic scene that includes talking, meaning, character, situation, and belief. Once this class is in the curriculum, you can throw in Maltese temple dancing if somebody thinks it will help.

I'm in enough trouble already, so I'm not going to talk about it.

15. The set is to do

Shhhh, don't tell, but sets and costumes are not sets and costumes, they are the actor's props. One of the best-kept secrets in acting is that it is a lot more about doing something than feeling something. Seen in this light, the set is the actor's jungle gym.

What does this actually mean? As soon as actors get on the set (or even when they see a rendering or model), they should make a list of what they can *do* with it. Here's an imaginary list:

1. It has a staircase so I could (depending on sightlines) sit on the stairs, slide down the bannister, dust the railing, jump over the railing, stamp up the steps to make a wonderful sound, toss a ball against the stairs.
2. It has a window with curtains so I could look out it, feel the texture of the curtains, draw on the window with my finger, pull up the blinds, whack the curtain against the wall to get rid of the dust, dust it (nobody dusts on stage anymore!), clean the window with my handkerchief, and wrap the curtains around me to see if they would make a good dress, just like Scarlett O'Hara did.
3. It has a door that opens and closes, so I could go out the door and then immediately come back in for the last line in the speech and then go out again and slam it (if, of course, it's slammable). I could lean against it exhausted. I could pound on it for emphasis (if, of

course, it's poundable). I could bang my head on it. I could slide down it in despair. I could lock it, unlock it, jimmy it with a hairpin, or scratch a booger off it with my fingernail. I could open and close it several times as punctuation for what I'm saying. I could kiss it because I love the house. I could open it to see if there are any rabid bears outside and close it with a sigh of relief.

4. If the set is an abstraction, I could slide, swing, climb, or run my hands over it. The set is a prop!

There are more goodies. There is furniture! What a cornucopia of behavior! I do an exercise where the actor shows me a dozen ways to sit in a chair. Make it two dozen. The same with the sofa. If it's a table you could... dust it (God, how I love dusting). You could sit on it (if it's sittable). You could write your name in the dust you didn't dust. You could put your feet on it. You could juggle the objects on it (and watch the prop master faint). You could play shuffleboard on it. You could draw on it, heck, you could lie down on it (ask first). You could steal something from it. You could pick off the remains of a fried egg. You could run your fingers along the grain, etc., etc.

The point here is that for the actor, the set is to do. Too many times I see plays where the set is merely a backdrop for the actor and never the twain shall meet. Actors are professional creatives and one of their creative acts is to find the to-do uses of the set. Now I realize this is going to give set designers indigestion and set off designerly panic attacks but the rule for the actor is common sense. No, you can't swing on the chandelier or eat the window seat (there's a wonderful novel by Harry Crews about a man eating a car). We're talking about the gentle and practical usage of the stage environment.

The costumes are props! (Author's note: my wife is a

costume designer so I will not suggest anything that will destroy my marriage.)

Costumes are an endless source of actor behavior and thus a treasure trove of the to-do. Let's start with contemporary clothes because that's what you'll be wearing the vast majority of the time, because nobody but the Shakespeare festivals has the money to do the classics. You have pockets and pockets contain Kleenex on which to blow your proboscis, credit cards with which to pick your teeth, and keys with which to amputate your infected finger. Clothes need brushing off (the sartorial version of dusting), hiking up, pulling down, and buttoning and unbuttoning, zipping and unzipping in various stages of romance. Baseball caps are for beating against your knee for no discernable reason. Shoes are for tying and untying while you relate the death of your pet gibbon. Ties and scarves are for tying and untying too. Belts are for tightening, underwear for pulling on, necklines for increasing or decreasing modesty, and gloves for pulling on with your teeth (well, maybe not). And everything you wear is for picking at while you think.

You are, dear actor, a walking prop table. Hemlines are for pulling down or hoisting up, depending. This could go on and on with slight detours into formal and swimwear. Don't just wear your clothes—do them. Most importantly, don't let my wife read this.

The bottom line in all of this is to view what's around you and on you as an integral aid to character and situation. Let's face it, if Nora had not had a door to slam on her way out of a repressive marriage in Ibsen's *A Doll's House,* who would remember the play? Okay, a few people, but you get the point.

Imagine plays without *doing*. Everybody would stand around with their hands at their sides reeking of "stage presence" but completely disengaged from the people and things around them. It wouldn't be a play—it would be a still life.

Sets and costumes are the answer to the anguished director's cry of "Don't just stand there, do something!" Think of your characters as in a state of doing. What you do is who you are; doing *is* character. Yes I know, you have props to do things with, but extend the definition of props to the rest of your theatrical world. There is obviously a difference between the performing arts and graphic arts other than one is two-dimensional and the other three. The second difference lies in the *doing* we have been chatting about. Good designers fully understand this and assist it.

So, here you are at the first tech wearing your glorious duds and standing dead center in the Parthenon. Now what? *Do.*

16. Why I hate emotions!

All right, all right, I don't really hate emotions. I even have them from time to time myself.

Horror, for one, when I see young actors presenting patented false emotions as if they were worth the price of admission. It is downright embarrassing. It turns the theatre into an endless Halloween, with actors dressing up in emotions they don't actually feel, much as they don't really believe they are vampires. Let me say this simply: directors and actors, stop encouraging and playing emotions you obviously don't feel. Cease and desist. Halt. Nevermore!

Actually, over a very long life, I have come to think that very few humans of my acquaintance actually like to feel emotions and when they do feel them, particularly negative emotions, it makes them angry, embarrassed, and often, silent. I know, I know, people do like to feel delighted, victorious, and loving. Luckily those emotions are easier to fake.

Example: when I teach acting in a university classroom, one of my chief pleasures is relating one on one with students. Several times a year when I was on the faculty at Santa Fe University of Art and Design, students would come to my office to discuss problems that were interfering with their work, progress, and lives. These would include family problems, relationship problems, medical problems, casting problems, etc. In the midst of delving into these problems a visitor sometimes might begin to cry, and though the tears proceed from a variety of circumstances, one thing is always clear: they don't want to be crying. As a matter of fact they hate crying, and they stop as soon as humanly possible. If they then cry again, they hate it as much the second time as the first. Having this emotion in this particular setting usually makes them angry with themselves. Of course this may be because I am their teacher and not their parent but as a parent I have seen the same reaction in my own children.

There are settings and situations in which emotions, particularly anger and grief, are allowed to flow freely and with no countering feeling of restraint, but I notice that the person feeling them sooner than later seeks solitude in which to continue their expression.

Expressed emotion is usually the last thing the person wants, a court of last resort, when all else fails. This is exactly how the actor should regard emotion—that which occurs when all control fails. Where I part company with the actor is when I don't see and feel this attempt to control what they feel before it breaks free into full expression on the stage. When there is no battle for control, the emotion seems like a desired result, or, to be blunt, phonier than a three dollar bill.

There is also a clear difference (a very, very clear difference) between faked crying, faked anger, faked despair, and even faked joy, and the real thing. The actor seeks the sound of the emotion and this concentration on the sound is obviously... well... faked. There are forms of non-realistic drama and acting where the theatrical conventions do not demand emotions that pass the test of "realism." Versions of realism, however, still dominate the American stage, and it is "emotion" within this context of realism that I here discuss.

So, in this somewhat realistic play, what are we to do instead of fake crying, fake anger, fake joy, etc.? Redouble your concentration on the *action,* raise the stakes on the action. If your roommate has stolen your pet iguana and perhaps has roasted and eaten it, don't show us how sad you are. Frantically seek the return of said iguana or restitution for same. If in the midst of trying to solve the problem semi-rationally, tears start running down your cheeks against your will, you have just produced an acting victory and should be carried from the theatre on the shoulders of the audience! Bravo and brava!

Let's talk about the actor's favorite emotion, anger. Actors love to play anger. It's the "strong emotion" rather than one of those "weak emotions." First of all actors get angry too soon and then they stay angry too long. On top of that they play angry too often. Sometimes way too often. I'm not talking about controlled or sublimated anger, which is cool. I'm talking about loud, sustained, seemingly endless anger which becomes the only sound I hear for an entire scene mixed in with a moment or two of sarcasm, if I'm lucky. Please don't. It flattens the scene, oversimplifies the scene, makes it almost impossible to follow, and makes me crazy. Male actors seem to equate such acting with macho, and women with diva-hood, and either way it just makes me wish I was in Sumatra. I have been witness to and participant in shouting matches and arguments in life and had I timed them, most lasted under a minute before control and the action reasserted themselves and these real people returned to having to convince instead of reveling in feeling powerful.

I had something of an ungovernable "anger" problem as a young man but I slowly got over it because it seldom to never got me what I wanted and was thus a useless exercise. This holds true not only for anger but a bevy of preferred stage emotions such as self-pity, desperation, profound love, depression, and stomach ache. I know, stomach ache isn't an emotion but it was fun to write.

People want things and they want to make sounds that help them get them. The only time sounding angry works is when you're employing people or you're the one paying the rent. Even then it doesn't get you anything in the long run. Most stage emotions are a form of venting and venting is a last resort in getting your way. Venting is what you do when you can't get what you want and out of frustration you rant, shout, and cry. Venting doesn't last long at all, and then human beings get back to the endless job of getting what they want in ways that may actually be successful.

One parting observation about anger. It works well as a warning shot. You can angrily shout "Don't touch that!" and it's effective as long as that's the end of it.

Fight back against emotion; don't sail into it for fun. Say to yourself, "I'm not going to cry, shout, or be depressed. I just won't, that's all. No way that is going to happen." And if you eventually lose that fight, against your better judgment and what it will probably cost you, that's fine. Just don't revel in it, okay? Don't. Particularly don't lose that battle if you just like sounding mad or can cry at will. I forgot to talk about crying. Actors are very proud of crying and they do it so often you just want to choke them.

Incontestable fact: audiences vastly prefer to see actors bravely attempt to solve a serious problem to seeing actors indulge themselves. Please tattoo this on your arm. If you eschew false emotion and devote yourself to problem solving you are far more likely to have a career. Would you like to have a career?

Last note, please don't manufacture your idea of the proper emotional sound because the word for an emotion is in your speech or your speech talks about an emotion. Let's say the speech is, "I have to tell you that, no matter what you think, I love you," Don't make the love sound on the word "love." Or "If you keep stealing my chickens I'll hate you." Don't make the hate sound on the word "hate." It seems absurd that I would even bring this up, right? Sorry, it happens all the time.

People don't come to the theatre to see your emotions. They come to the theatre to see you solve your problems and get emotional when you can't. Tattoo that on your other arm.

Playing the emotion is just terrible and none of the paying customers are taken in. It's like watching kids play dress up. Unfortunately you're not as cute as a kid.

You are absolved of worrying about forcing emotions on stage. Go in peace.

17. The over-clarifying, too emphatic, psychologically one-note, terrible, horrible, no good actor

It's a good thing to understand the predominant quality in a major role, but it's a bad thing to overplay it. Major roles are called "major" because they usually get a lot of stage time, and their predominant quality usually sticks out like a sore thumb.

Let us say you get cast as Romeo. Romeo is a lover. Exactly. If Romeo isn't profoundly, strikingly, astoundingly in love, the play won't work. I saw a production where Romeo was a hunky, star quarterback sort of lover who seemed determined to get and have Juliet but was more involved in "having" than in "loving," and that clearly didn't work. On the other hand I've seen a dozen Romeos who were so busy lyricizing their love that you wanted to tie them up backstage so they couldn't make another rhapsodizing entrance.

Yes and yes again, you need to identify the characteristic without which the story won't be clear. Yes, the Heathers are bad girls. They treat others abominably, and the film and musical are careful to make that clear. The potential problem: that major, driving necessity can be so overplayed we have nothing to see that we haven't seen five minutes earlier. Don't ride the major quality until it dies under you like an exhausted horse in a brutal Western. *The Revenant* comes to mind.

It's sort of like adoring the color green, not realizing

there are a hundred shades of green until after you have painted the whole house emerald green, making it only fit for leprechauns. Now is this really, truly, honestly an acting problem? I mean it's pretty obvious, right? It doesn't actually happen, does it?

It does, yes. You've probably done it. I've done it. It isn't that we're lazy, though unfortunately that's part of it. It could be that we've been in the hands of directors making the same mistake. It might be that you haven't been in an acting program that places enough emphasis on script analysis.

Digression

Script analysis. After fifteen years of teaching acting full-time I fully realize there is only so much acting you can teach without constantly pairing it with unpacking the script. I also think that students and teachers generally prefer being up on their feet acting to sitting down and thinking about acting. Thought, however, must be in the mix and can't always be done on your feet. It's a teaching dilemma.

Trick question: does your acting curriculum have both a beginning and advanced script analysis class? (Or even one?) How about that college program you're considering?

We resume our journey

All right. Romeo and Juliet contains as great a "love, love, love, love, love" speech as has ever been written. Romeo has met Juliet at the dance and gone literally crazy over her. Afterward he hops over her garden wall and hangs out, hoping she will come out on her balcony so he can say "love, love, love" to her. He then does the famous "But soft! What light through yonder window breaks?" speech. There is not a sentence in this nice long speech that doesn't drip "love" like a honeycomb in a heat wave. It's twenty-four Shakespearean lines long. I have listened to actors love it to death, literally. They vibrate with this super-obvious love for twenty-four endless lines. OMG.

Confronted with this lyric feast of language, how does the actor make his feelings clear without overdoing it? In other words, how does the actor give us the basic through line of the speech without treating us as if we were in kindergarten learning our colors? What keeps the speech "green" without it all being "emerald green?"

1. Danger. He's a Montague, she's a Capulet. These families hate each other big time. He's a Montague in a Capulet's backyard after midnight. He could easily get skewered like a kebab. Play "love, love, love," but watch your back. He has a heightened sense of danger even in the midst of his lyricism.

2. She flirted with him at the dance and probably enjoyed the thrill of breaking the rules. Will she do the same when she is in her nightie and they are alone in the dark? Play "love, love, love" but be unsure of her returning your feelings. Maybe Romeo's out of his league.

3. Play "love, love, love" but he doesn't have much time. The nurse is in Juliet's room and may catch them at any moment. He's got to get it done.

4. Play "love, love, love" but worry you're not cute enough. Be worried you'll lose the Montague/Capulet argument that's bound to come up. Try a little insecurity.

5. Fact: we are no longer Elizabethan actors in an Elizabethan society handling verse like the Elizabethans did. We can't do what they did; people would think we were

crazy. For the contemporary actor there's the dilemma of keeping the verse and images together in a cogent way and at the same time making all this great stuff up at that very moment. Play "love, love, love" but for God's sake think! Thinking gives "love, love, love" a different set of tonalities.

You get all this, right? You have to know what the basic necessity of the scene is for your character and get that done, but it's not a straight Red Bull; it's a beverage order that might challenge a seasoned barista. Not letting the circumstances affect the basic feeling turns it into tonal acting, where you play the love tone, or, the hate tone, or the mad tone, or the hurt tone throughout, instead of making sure the circumstances and your character's psychology modulate the tone from moment to moment.

The scene, and even the play, may demand you make one thing about this character incontrovertibly clear, but make sure you play all the colors of that one thing. After you've been rehearsing for a while, make sure you're not teaching kindergarten with your performance. Don't act the role as if we don't get it. Show us all the things about what we get that we haven't thought of yet.

18. What to do when things go badly

In the long and rewarding acting career I hope you have, it will be rare (as in football) that you go undefeated. As a matter of fact, every acting performance has its ups and downs, its delicious small victories and its intractable problems. So what do we do when it's going south? The answer is simple and concise: don't generalize. Don't say, "I'm incredibly terrible in act two," because act two is filled with hundreds if not thousands of acting moments, some you do well and some of which are works in progress. Don't generalize!

But if you are in a state and can't keep from generalizing, here's primarily what you are talking about: the super objective or, in plainer terms, what your character wants above all in act two. Yes, I know, sometimes the character wants a lemonade and sometimes a puppy and sometimes to be left alone, but what's the big "want?" The sustaining "want?" The want into which all the little wants fit? That might be that Jimmy would love her, or that she could kill Frank and get away with it, or that she could move to Miami and study marine biology. The big want! You may be playing "thirsty" or "lonely," but lemonade won't get you to Miami.

What's wrong with your performance that is making you edgy or unhappy is that you haven't determined the larger goal into which lemonade and the puppy can fit. I stopped writing this article twice already, once to make tea and once to fold laundry. But while I drank and folded, I was thinking about how to say what I wanted to say. When the overall *want* is missing you will always have that frustrated feeling that your acting isn't interesting and may be just a little bit soulless. Your acting isn't terrible, but it feels passionless because very few people are truly fulfilled by lemonade. Work on the larger problem and the smaller ones will make the larger ones clearer. Stop moping and go big.

Now, the second solution to your sense of unease is the arc. Your acting has to go on a journey and we don't pay forty dollars to see you go from Toledo to Toledo. Hamlet starts out feeling terrible because he hates his mother marrying so soon after his father's death and he suspects his mother's new husband actually murdered his father and he's not doing anything about it. He's so upset with himself that he's suicidal. His journey is from this self-loathing aimlessness to pulling himself together and giving up his life in the fight to avenge his father. Call it the trip from debilitating indecision to fulfilling action.

What's the trip your character is taking? Your acting can't be the same at the end as it was in the beginning, and the middle is a mix of both. Quite seriously, when your acting isn't going well it's because you are distracted by the little stuff and have lost track of the super objective and the arc. It's like eating a few pretzels and peanuts and wondering why you're still hungry.

"Okay," I can hear you saying, "but the little stuff is driving me crazy." Fine, let's talk about the little stuff.

1. "I feel boring." Solution: pursue whatever your character wants in the short term passionately. If you want a kiss, play it as if you'll die if you don't get it. Then I guarantee you, you won't feel boring. Really.
2. "I don't feel attractive." Yeah, yeah, yeah—passionate people are attractive. Play passionately.

3. "I can't work with Samantha. She just isn't giving me anything." Befriend Samantha. Bring her a homemade blueberry muffin. Compliment her shoes. Once she doesn't think you hate her, confide that you think you aren't doing a good job in act one, scene three, and can the two of you talk over that scene while eating chocolate-covered cherries you will provide? Figure out with Sam what the scene is about, what each character wants the outcome to be, and what they want from each other. Actors who haven't had, or feel they can't have, that conversation are likely to think things aren't going well.

4. You don't like that you are just standing there, which feels naked and profoundly uninteresting. Obviously, to feel profoundly uninteresting isn't very nice. This is one of the small problems that can wreak havoc with the actor's sense of how it's going. The solution is behavior. You're not doing anything, so frankly, you have this itchy feeling that you don't exist, Do something! Retie your shoelace. Adjust your earrings. Change your seated position so you're more comfortable. Take out a stick of chewing gum, unwrap it, and pop it in your mouth. Check your hands to make sure you cleaned your fingernails. Scratch the mosquito bite. Do something! Humans are involved in behaviors even while they are waiting to hear the sentence at their murder trial. They behave even while their husband says he's leaving her. Behaviors ground the actor, release acting tension, define character, create realism, and involve the audience. To be blunt, you may not know how to improve your performance, but you do know how to tie your shoe. Doing something that restores your confidence onstage immediately makes you attractive and will feed and release your creativity. Really.

Finally, one more piece of advice. When you are doubting yourself, your work and your talent, and are considering a career as a rabbit whisperer rather than acting, and you open this Friday, and everything you do seems horrible—don't generalize; work specifically. Remember the old phrase, "Light a candle; don't curse the darkness?" You hate act two, scene two, which runs from page thirty-two to thirty-seven? Don't worry about the length. Work on solving the first six lines on page thirty-two, then move on. Sonny, you can't fix it all. But each thing you fix will make it easier to fix the next.

Generalizations don't solve acting problems. Tattoo that on your hand. Fix this and then fix that. After a few fixes, your confidence alone will fix other stuff. *Trust me.* Nobody ever got all of Hamlet "right." Stop worrying about "the whole thing" and fix the first six lines on page thirty-two—that is what to do when things are going badly.

II
PERSPECTIVES ON ACTOR TRAINING

19. The conversation

Many of you have already had, or at least begun, "the conversation." This is the talk during which your parents bluntly, gently, and/or sadly try to talk you out of majoring in acting, musical theatre, costume or set design, or technical work in college. It is well meant, a product of how much they love you and a desire to keep you from harm. It is by any measure a good talk to have.

It is in the main an economic conversation. Your parents want you to have shelter and food and they would prefer you didn't come back to live with them after you graduate. It is also grounded in a definition of success and happiness that you may or may not share.

I spent several years teaching acting in the performing arts department of an undergraduate program that granted B.A. and B.F.A. degrees. When parents accompanied their children on exploratory visits, they usually asked me for a few minutes of my time to discuss Aurora or Benjamin's "future." Aurora and Benjamin looked very uncomfortable.

These meetings would come to the point very, very quickly. "What job opportunities, Mr. Jory, will be available to Aurora upon graduation with her acting degree?" My life passed before my eyes. I was poignantly aware of what my college would like me to say at this moment. They would have liked me to tell the story of the young actor who graduated in musical theatre two years ago, moved to New York and less than a month later was appearing on Broadway in *The Book of Mormon.* Or the one of the actress who was at that moment the star of, get this, one of the most popular television series in Japan. The college would have liked me to talk about all the acting opportunities available on cruise ships and how young actors can do voiceovers for cartoons and teach corporate executives to give a speech. Sometimes I use these diversionary tactics and sometimes I tell the truth.

The truth is that Aurora and Benjamin will get all sorts of job offers, and practically none of them will be acting jobs. When I related this information, the room would go cold. Icicles formed on the parents ears. "You see," I would say, "very few young actors get good paying acting jobs between twenty and twenty-five. This is called the 'gap.' During this period young actors work in retail sales, catering, restaurant work, etc., and they do non-paying non-union acting in the evening. And you, dear parents, will probably be called on to provide whatever support you can."

There would be a pause. A parent leaned forward, making serious eye contact. She said, "So we're paying thirty-five thousand dollars a year so Aurora, degree in hand, can work in the fast food industry?" Good question, huh? And the answer is, "Yes. Probably. On the other hand somebody walks out of every casino in America, every night, twenty-five thousand dollars richer than when they came in." Then I tell the story about the young actress and *The Book of Mormon.*

Let's come clean here. To defend acting or set design as a sensible economic choice in the twenty-first century in America is... well... untenable. The parents are secretly sure that's true even before they sit down. It is, of course, possible to make a great deal of money as an actor, but that is almost an accidental outcome. You cannot assume it or plan for it. Acting, I believe, is a passion, not a profession, and my secret belief is that having a passion is an extraordinary piece of good luck. But for passion to trump rational, practical behavior is very hard for a parent to accept. Very hard. Very frightening. It makes it much more complicated if not impossible to defend the child against life's difficulties, the very process we believe is a parent's responsibility. Thus, "the conversation."

The good news for parents is that ninety percent of the time their child is curious about acting, they are flirting with the idea of it, but time shows they are not passionate about acting, and from the parents' point of view, they ultimately "get well." To parents having the conversation I would simply counsel patience. Most people have the sense to come in out of the cold.

But not everyone. The ones with the passion are not economically driven; insecurity they find bearable, material possessions are nice but not crucial, they are (and I am truly sorry to say this) not necessarily driven by family values. What they want is to act. And there is nothing for a parent to do but love them for it because that's the way it's going to go down.

Most people who get theatre degrees are out of the profession within five years, and all but the diehards in ten. They find other paths and build productive lives, families, and useful careers. Very few become doctors, lawyers, and engineers, but that was never in the cards really, was it?

Among the diehards there's another shakeout in their mid-thirties, leaving only the diehard-diehards. By then there are only two kinds of actors left: actors who love it and are making a good or great living, and actors who love it so much it will never matter what they're making.

Parents can take some comfort in this: I have personally never heard of an actor who has become homeless or starved to death, and I know innumerable actors who love their lives and are not troubled by driving used cars. An undergraduate theatre degree is not a death knell. It's just a bumpy process with some downsides, if I were braver I would say the following things to parents and their children in "the conversation."

1. Why on earth isn't this young person going to a community college for two years? Cost-effective doesn't even begin to describe it! At the community college the actor will get the rudiments of what used to be called a liberal education, and every community college does plays. Plus in my endless career of teaching acting, I don't find that eighteen- and nineteen-year-olds are usually ready to learn much about acting. Acting classes just wash over them like a warm shower.

2. When they transfer, do the research necessary to make sure they are going to a school with a record of graduates having professional careers and that the acting faculty has worked professionally. The third thing: look at photographs of productions at the school. Do the sets and costumes look cool? This is usually a sign that the acting program is well supported by the university.

3. After that, I recommend that parents stop involving themselves in "the conversation" and let this thing play out. It will turn out all right and it's going to take some time. Enjoy the fact that you have raised a child who has a passion. People with passions lead richer lives than people without them. If you keep pushing people with passions to give them up, they won't like you.

So, to the people on both sides of the conversation I say, stay flexible. Give in a little to get a little. And to the parents I say, talking economics to a person who desperately wants to give acting a try is usually.., well... unproductive.

You could force your dependent child to do something she doesn't want to do. How does that parenting method usually work out for you? We can't scare an interest in acting out of our children by worrying them about having high-paying jobs when they graduate. They won't, and so what?

20. Do your homework

Oh dear. Choosing a college drama program. How? The most desirable schools are next to impossible to get into. The others are likely to hustle you like a star quarterback. The country is awash in theatre programs and to survive, those programs must have students. Now as this is an acting book, I'm going to talk about acting programs, not design/tech programs. I am, I fear, opinionated and only tangentially rational on the entire subject.

Here's the rub: only one in twenty (or fewer) collegiate drama students will still be in the profession fifteen years after graduation. The others will be leading productive lives and sometimes doing avocational acting. The people who make a living as actors are either in the top five percent of the talent, are devastatingly, conventionally beautiful, or (somebody wins the lottery every day) both.

Now let's suppose, for giggles, that you aren't in the top five percent and have more of an ordinary look. What exactly are you doing in an acting program, and what are you likely to get out of it?

- It's what you enjoy.
- You have no idea how talented you are, so this way, you hope, you'll find out.
- You like to be part of a group, and theatre guarantees that.

- You're creative; theatre is creative. Bingo.
- What aren't you getting out of it?
- Well, it's probably not going to strengthen your intellectual powers or your general trove of information, or tremendously increase your understanding of the world around you. A college that needs students might say it will, but they are fibbing.
- You aren't meeting people who are very different from yourself, because college theatre departments keep you busy from nine a.m. until eleven p.m. six days a week.
- You won't take many classes in other areas, for the same reason.
- And, most likely, you won't be able to make a living at it until you're twenty-five or so. Thus you are, at least for a time, taking a vow of poverty.

Worried? Very sensible. Some will point out, of course, that there are intangible benefits to theatre training, such as poise, presence, learning how to work hard, communication skills, teamwork, etc. And that's true. All very helpful in the hotel industry, retail, advertising, and working on cruise ships. Is this turning you on?

All right, am I saying you will ruin your life by studying acting? Of course not. It may, however, create serious problems with your finances, if you care about that. I didn't. Let us not forget, though, that many acting students come out of college with significant debt. A survey of recent acting class seniors showed that more than half would graduate from a B.F.A. program with between $30,000 and $100,000 in student loan debt. This amounts to a bruising problem for young actors who will be fortunate to make fifteen thousand a year in the field on graduation.

But enough with practicality. There would probably be no actors if practicality was a defining measure. You are going to major in acting, come what may, and I might as well shut up about it. Where?

First of all, are you looking for a conservatory program (all acting, all the time) or a more conventional B.F.A. program (acting about half the time)? The only undergraduate programs the profession gives a damn about are all conservatory programs, and those are Juilliard, Carnegie Mellon, and North Carolina School of the Arts, though reputable programs like Boston University, Cal Arts, Minnesota, and Syracuse deeply resent it. All the rest are either okay or not okay, and it would take a book to sort them out. If you apply to Juilliard, Carnegie Mellon, or North Carolina School of the Arts and are accepted, it's a sign you're talented. There are hundreds of serious acting programs, though, and good actors have come from almost all of them, but not in bunches.

What to look for:

- Are the teaching staff working professionals? You would probably not choose to learn engineering from people who have never been engineers.
- Is it in a city where you can see good theatre? You need to see good theatre.
- Visit the damn school. Students who enroll in acting programs without having seen what actually goes on and having talked to the students are in for some very nasty surprises.
- See a production there. If the production doesn't excite you, how can the training?
- Ask about the number of productions per semester and the number of acting students in the four-year program.

Let's say there are four productions, averaging ten actors, and there are ninety actors in the department. That means half the actors won't be cast in any given semester.

- How good are the actors in the production? You need to be surrounded by talent.
- Do you judge the acting classes to be practical? Or can't you figure out why they are doing what they are doing? Acting is not really very complicated. Are they demystifying acting or creating theology? If they spend considerable time throwing imaginary balls back and forth, run for the hills.
- Do you feel comfortable in the college's theatre department or do you have the strange feeling you have joined a cult?
- Do you like the atmosphere in the class, and does the teacher energize you?
- Are the students happy to be there?
- What is the curriculum? Get the handbook, your favorite beverage, and a Boston cream pie and examine it. Are there voice classes, is there physical training, what do the acting classes actually teach? How many acting classes do you take in four years? Oh, and what are the class sizes? An acting class with more than sixteen people in it is a joke.

Do your homework. Don't accept a college on trust. Are you sure you shouldn't get your general education classes at a community college, which is way less expensive, and then transfer? (Make certain the credits will be transferable before you attempt this.)

Plan to take a hard look at yourself after your sophomore year. If you have serious doubts about your talent and marketability, should you change course? If you do two years only to find out you are not an actor, are there other courses of study in that college that attract you?

Do your due diligence in finding a school. Don't take anything on faith. Know exactly what you'll be taught, and check out the cafeteria's food and the quality of the student body. You are the consumer. There are good programs and terrible programs. Care deeply about your decision. You can make this work for yourself.

In a sensible country of this size, there would be far fewer colleges with acting schools that would have great professional faculties, and they would be extremely selective. We, however, don't live there.

21. What now?

Let's talk about a career as an actor. I'm going to invent a seventeen-year-old high school student from Albuquerque, New Mexico, named Sandy Ortega. Sandy has just graduated from high school and has been accepted by the University of Washington in Seattle as an undergraduate acting student. Here's our conversation.

Jon: Sandy, I know you're serious about pursuing a career as an actress. What can I tell you?

Sandy: Does it matter when I graduate from TJW whether I have a B.A. or a B.F.A.? Professionally, I mean?

Jon: Not really. In all the years I've worked in the profession I've never looked to see which degree the person auditioning for me had. Once in the profession it's the talent and accomplishments of the person in front of us that matter.

Sandy: Does it matter where I got my undergraduate degree?

Jon: Hmmm. To a minor degree. In the profession we've heard of Juilliard, Carnegie Mellon, and North Carolina School of the Arts. There are many more good programs, but they don't penetrate the professional mind set. It's mainly *what* you've learned, not *where* you learned.

Sandy: What about graduate school? Is that truly useful or even necessary?

Jon: If you are in the top two percent of the country's talent or so beautiful or handsome that people faint when you walk through Target, then you should probably empty your bank account and take the next covered wagon to L.A. or N.Y.C. and forget the M.F.A. If you are a more ordinary mortal (talented, but not a god; pleasant-looking, but not Mr. or Ms. Universe), then you need to consider graduate school, for several reasons. Here are two. One, most people coming out of undergraduate programs are really not professional-caliber actors and need both more training and seasoning to be competitive. And two, there is what we call "the gap." Most actors don't start to get jobs until they are twenty-four or so. This means if you are twenty or twenty-one when you get your diploma from the Bismark, North Dakota School of Wheat and Performance, then you are staring at three or four pretty tough (even bleak) years before the job opportunities beckon. What to do? Remember grad school? The top programs offer excellent training, networking, and a morning-till-midnight focus on what you love to do. Enough said.

Sandy: If I decide to take off for L.A. or New York or Chicago or wherever, how much money should I have in that bank account you told me to empty?

Jon: You want money so you can get your bearings, find and pay for housing, get an agent, and have time to audition before you start working twelve-hour shifts for United Parcel to pay your bills and provide you with pizza. You should have ten thousand dollars in your saddle bag. This means a lot of people spend a year working after they snag that B.F.A. before they launch. Just the way it is.

Sandy: I know someone who didn't do grad school but resettled in Seattle and did eleven nonunion productions in two years and then moved to New York. Is that a plan?

Jon: Yes. Seattle, Chicago, Houston, Washington, Austin, Minneapolis, San Francisco, Philadelphia—any city with a fairly large population base has a blue-million non-Equity theatres. You'll be working a day job and acting at night and living like a medieval priest. Better store up your energy! Remember, don't get too comfortable there. Even if you become the theatre diva of Sarasota, you need to pack up your kit bag after a couple of years and go try L.A. or N.Y.C. Know how many actors actually make a full-time living in Seattle? Maybe three dozen.

Sandy: Okay, let's get real. What grad schools are the best?

Jon: Are you trying to get me killed by a secret operative of Wallaby College in Wisconsin? Don't tell anybody what I say here. Consider location. Good grad schools in the acting centers of America (L.A. and N.Y.C.) allow you to start building a career even while you are in school. We're talking Yale, Juilliard, NYU, Columbia, Cal Arts, USC, UCLA, plus schools all the way out of L.A. like University of California, San Diego and University of California, Irvine. There are another two dozen excellent programs outside these centers such as U. of Washington, U. of Tennessee, Florida State, Rutgers, SMU, PlayMakers Rep., U. of Virginia, and several more. Check to see what financial support is offered. At some schools (and you know who you are) you could come out with over a hundred thousand in student debt—that is ugly. Do not accept a graduate school until you do your due diligence. What support is offered? What acting methods are pursued? Is there good physical and voice work? How many years is the program and is it a professional faculty and what is their résumé? Plus, if you hate winter, why are you training for three years in Chicago?

Sandy: And when I get out of graduate school?

Jon: Hope you have first-rate skills and good karma and head for the places where actors make a living.

Sandy: Thank you. I think I'll go lie down now.

22. An argument for democratic casting

There is a difficult problem in many American college undergraduate theatre programs that is not addressed, not because it isn't recognized but because finding a solution is difficult, both psychologically and practically.

It is this: many acting majors graduate from college programs without ever having appeared in a main stage, faculty-directed play. What!? People pay their tuition, do their classwork, and in four years never get cast? What could justify that? One hears that "casting is not a right but a privilege." In other words, proper acting is not included in your acting tuition.

This seems a bit odd, doesn't it? One would suppose that you learn skills in classes and then practice them onstage. If we asked you to learn how to play tennis from lectures and films in class but without guaranteed court time ("That's a privilege, pal"), you would call it absurd. You likely would not attend that school.

If prospective students applied the same standard to college theatre programs, it would be a disaster! Programs would close right and left. Faculty would have to work behind the counter at Arby's. Million-dollar facilities would rot unused.

To avoid this big—budget disaster-movie fate, many college programs don't say much about casting policies in their recruitment and marketing efforts. You won't find out the hard truth until you arrive.

This situation is not, however, a scam. It's an intractable problem for colleges and their faculties. At its root lies, as usual, money. Secondarily, the problem involves "talent" and how talent develops. And finally, it's psychological.

Let's start with money. Most (but not all) undergraduate theatre programs are short-staffed, because theatre, in addition to class work, entails *productions*. Sets, lights, sound, props, and costumes all require equipment and personnel that the Medieval Literature department simply does not have to contend with. These expenses make theatre programs, well... expensive. They also make other college programs jealous. "How come those theatre nerds get larger faculties than we creative writing nerds?" The answer, of course, is that carpenters and seamsters cost more money than copy paper, right? But even with this relatively larger faculty, only so many productions are possible. A costume shop manager in a college teaches classes *and* spends hundreds of hours building and altering costumes. They also oversee four to eight productions a year.

The practical limitations on the number of productions, and thus roles, inevitably create casting problems. Hence: "casting is a privilege, not a right."

Let's take a quick mathematical review of why you may never be cast. We'll call our college Watahootchie University, operating in the State of Despair. The administration decrees that, to maintain the program, the Watahootchie Theatre Department must admit 120 acting majors. They also see the production department's understaffing as a "financial necessity." These overworked staffers exhibit monumental goodwill by undertaking three major productions a semester, for a total of six a year. Each of the six plays would have to cast twenty actors (remember this number) per production so that all 120 students could have one—and *no more* than one—role a year. Therefore, no single student, no matter how talented, accomplished, and responsible—may have two or more roles each year. This, by the way, makes the most talented and accomplished student actors cranky, so they transfer to other, less democratic programs. But that aside ...

A cast of *twenty* in every production? This is a problem because, out in the professional world, practically no theatre can payroll a cast of that size, so playwrights very sensibly write for a maximum of six actors. Casting for twenty means producing plays written before 1970, where theatre economics were not so bloody strict. So how to choose among these older, often less-than-relevant scripts? Well, you could do any of the great classics written before actors unionized. Shakespeare, Sophocles, or Farqhuar productions, with their large casts and extravagantly dear costumes, demand first-rate direction, not to mention acting performances exceeding most undergraduate capabilities. Most departments won't do more than one a year. So Watahootchie plays offer an average twelve-actor cast per play (times six), which comes to seventy-two roles per year. This leaves forty-eight students a year with no fully supported, mainstage part.

Now, mathematically speaking, over four years everyone might be able to share the spotlight—if it weren't for those directors wishing to cast the most talented students, those "usual suspects." Directing plays is the only obviously competitive part of a theatre faculty's job, where their work will be compared with other faculty members' work. Now don't tell me it isn't—it *is*. Only Mother Teresa wouldn't care, and maybe Buddha and Gandhi. Are they on your faculty? Not at Watahootchie. At Watahootchie, about ten to fifteen of the 120 student actors get cast in almost every play because, at that point, their talents are better developed. This screws up the democratic math entirely. A good performance makes the director look good. An inadequate performance makes the director look inadequate.

At Watahootchie, that means the better developed actors hog the good roles, and the actors who aren't going to really develop until they are twenty-five (if ever) may never get cast in four years. Thus the sound logic that, to improve as an actor, you must act in plays directed by the best directors available—wearing an actual costume, upon an actual set, with actual props and an actual sound score—is set aside by the absurd notion that acting in plays "isn't a right but a privilege." In other words, because of these knotty issues, Watahootchie is kind of fibbing about the quality of their training and whether (if you don't become one of the usual suspects) you actually get your substantial money's worth. Poor Watahootchie has no desire to cheat you. (They are honorable people.) But, hey, guess what? *They are.*

In Watahootchie's defense, they recognize the problem. They give it the old college try. Because directors shun democratic casting, a bunch of other plays spring up—without costumes or sets, directed by student novices in hallways and broom closets, without faculty oversight. This way, there are more roles, and the school year doesn't devolve into an underfunded staging of the French Revolution. Here I must make some claims that invoke common sense and are not strictly verifiable. Here's one: plays inadequately directed without working costumes, sets, and props are not valued by student actors as much as mainstage productions. The cast may not tell the faculty this, but they know a hawk from a handsaw. They ain't fooled. And unfortunately (here's another one): terrible productions don't make you better. My forty years of work have made this conclusion undeniable, if subjective.

Goodness glory, what to do? My only conclusion is that democratic casting should be a required standard in undergraduate acting programs. Casting could be tracked statistically to provide all majors with at least two decent roles over the four-year period. As casting proceeds over the year, directors could review a list of those not yet cast. It would be mandatory for directors to cast underserved seniors. Juniors would take second priority, and so forth.

Would this seriously affect the quality of the productions? Well, the cold, hard truth is that even if did, it is still fair, decent, and necessary to the students. Meanwhile, there will always be pleasant surprises, and anyway, the two or three leading roles could still be filled by the usual suspects. I seriously doubt that audiences, who fully realize they are not attending professional work, would notice or object.

Schools adhering to such a discipline would gain recruiting advantage by publicizing their more democratic casting policy. Students and parents would, of course, react very positively, thereby boosting the theatre department's reputation and visibility. It is really hard to conceive of a downside, other than reining in directors' competitive natures (which can and should be done). In the classroom, we would not for a minute think it ethical to only teach our best students. In what way is casting different?

I do not suggest democratic casting to master's degree programs in acting. Those are students committed to careers, and the competitive nature of the profession is something they must confront and deal with.

For undergraduates, parents, and plain old ethical necessity, I humbly suggest this reform.

III.

GETTING WORK, AND OTHER PROFESSIONAL CONSIDERATIONS

III.

23. What they are thinking

The books written about auditioning would fill a small warehouse, but they never really tell you what the people working the audition are feeling and thinking. Allow me to remedy that. Having run two theatres and *pest*-directed over the course of (oh, dear!) forty years, I can lift the curtain on your auditioners.

Here are five things they are feeling.

1. Desperate. They need to cast this part in a way that will make them look good.
2. Bored. Most auditions aren't very good, but the auditioners have to look like they are fascinated.
3. Hungry. They often wish you were chicken salad on rye.
4. Worried. They haven't seen the right person yet, and they have to catch a plane to Boise in two hours.
5. Confused. They aren't exactly sure what they are looking for.

And here are five things they are thinking.

1. Is she ever going to get out of that chair?
2. If he keeps playing emotions he doesn't feel, I'll have to stab him with my mechanical.

3. He's nineteen years old. What on earth makes him think he can play Falstaff?
4. He showed me everything he had in the first thirty seconds, and there's five more minutes to go!
5. I wonder why she didn't wash her hair.

Here are the five biggest sins in auditioning.

1. You don't understand what the scene or piece is really about. No amount of style and flash can cover that up.
2. There is hardly any connection between the brain and the body. The impulses upstairs don't move the body downstairs.
3. This actor is possessed of the terminal "cutes." What would I have to do to stop her from being "darling?"
4. Oh, my God, will he ever stop shouting!
5. Auditioning is a competitive event, and you obviously haven't prepared enough to compete.

Those watching you can really only detect the following five things.

1. The character in this audition doesn't seem to want things; she only wants to show things.
2. He's uncomfortable and scared. This is more about actor fear than it is about acting.
3. She has a workable body/no body.
4. She has/doesn't have a voice I could stand to listen to for two hours.

5. Her understanding/non-understanding of the psychology of the character in the situation is smart/dumb.
6. He has charm/no charm.

(Okay, I lied when I said there were five.)

We should probably talk about charm for a minute, because it's seldom articulated as a necessary adjunct to successful acting. Charm is what we call the quality that makes us want to spend an evening in the actor's company.

1. Really smart people charm with their intelligence.
2. Inward and outward beauty charms.
3. The confidence that "I am enough" charms. It is the actor's sense that they are enough and have enough to be worth looking at and listening to. They believe in themselves.
4. The fact that the actor moves well charms.
5. The actor's variety in the role charms.

Most people who get roles possess at least three of these forms that charm takes.

Now, a little more talk about the psychology of your audition. If it's late in the day and they still haven't found anyone to cast, they pay very close attention to you. If they have already identified two people they could cast, they are simply measuring you against those two people—it's like the Final Four in basketball. If you see them looking down at your résumé during your audition, it's not a good sign. It usually means they are already bored with you and need something to do. It could also mean they like you and wonder if you've worked with anyone they know. Unfortunately, it's more often number one than number two.

Don't get your underwear in a twist if they stop you before you are done. It could mean they love your work and don't need to see more, or they don't like your work and don't want to see more. In either case, you won't know which until a casting decision is made. If they are rude, it is because there are rude people in this world, not because you deserve it. You can't control what they think. They might not cast you because you remind them of their first wife. You can only control the work you do. If you have done the work you wanted to do, go home and forget the audition.

Good work will eventually result in getting cast. I asked a young actress (a good one) what her ratio of auditions to job offers was. She said one out of twenty. If you haven't even done twenty real auditions yet, you are needlessly worrying.

Here are five ways to improve your auditioning.

1. Play what the character wants.
2. Let your mind move your body.
3. Show us some variety.
4. Practice.
5. Now practice some more.

24. How do you feel?

Feelings. The actor has a lot of them in the work process, and managing those feelings is a crucial part of a career. No, I'm not talking about the feelings of the actor/character in performance. I'm talking about your feelings in auditions, rehearsal, and the dressing room. Doing a play is to ride an emotional rollercoaster, with all the requisite ups, downs, and curves. Are you "enough?" Will you (in your own mind) "succeed" or "fail?"

I won't spend a lot of time on the audition process. First there's the excitement about the coming test. We all enjoy those feelings. Then there's the nerve-jangling tidal wave of feelings about possible failure. You haven't gotten a part in the last three auditions and it hurt. Now you're feeling the fear and pain of experiencing more of the same.

Stop it! Anticipating the sting of audition failure can keep you from preparing. It's the old "If I don't try, I haven't really failed" syndrome. The problem there is obvious, right? If you don't try, you won't succeed, and it's the success of getting the role you profoundly want.

Concentrate on the work of preparing. Congratulate yourself on having the will power to put in the hours. Try to keep your mind away from anticipating the result. Be proud of yourself for doing the work. You're creating. You're making something, and this pleasure of "making something" is one of the great joys in acting. Remember, you can't control how others feel about your work, but you can control the work itself.

Also keep in mind that professionals only book one out of twenty (or thirty) auditions. You must not let "audition fears" infect audition preparation. It's indulgent. Stop indulging.

But here's the good news, you got the part, now the rollercoaster really leaves the station (and I'm petrified of rollercoasters). You pick up your script and your inner critic has a field day. And so does your ego. You only got a small part. You didn't want to play Guildenstem, you wanted to play Hamlet. Or, conversely, how am I ever going to play Hamlet? I'm not ready, I'm not good enough. Public failure rushes toward you like an oncoming train.

You need to refocus yourself on process, not result. You need to stop projecting and enjoy the work itself. In a very, very long career as a director, I have only two or three times gotten "the success I deserve," and I've directed over two hundred plays!

First of all, acting is richly complex and you are going to make a lot of mistakes. Mistakes cannot be avoided. An actor makes hundreds (if not thousands) of decisions in the creation of a major role. The overwhelming odds are that, on reflection, you'll regret a good many, and others, rightly or wrongly, won't be admired or may be actively disliked. That's not failure, that's a given in the profession. It's the way it *is*.

Take comfort in the scientific method. You get as much or more crucial information from what doesn't work as you do from what does. The fact of the matter is you're not going to do everything "right," and that's as true as that gravity will pull a ball thrown in the air back to the ground. Getting your underwear in an agonizing twist over criticism is like arguing with gravity. The more you fear "mistakes," the more you'll make.

Believe me, if your perfectionism makes mistakes

as painful as snakebite, acting is the wrong profession to choose. God willing you can laugh at yourself. Trying to avoid mistakes by not making the constant decisions demanded will compromise your acting and your creativity, which is likely to hang back like a beaten dog. Go for it! Let the mistakes fall where they may.

Simply put, if you perceive the natural ups and downs of creativity as your personal failures, you're not going to take the risk necessary to creation. If no one has told you that creativity is often painful, they've been holding out on you. You are going to feel lower lows than the accountant, and much higher highs.

One last reality: there's a director (remember her?) and the process of working with a director includes the pointing out of your "mistakes." You are going into a profession where someone is going to say, or imply, "don't do that" on a regular, daily basis and that will sting. If you go into boxing you're going to be hit. If you become a ballerina you're going to have painful foot problems. It comes with the territory, don't obsess over it. It stings but it usually doesn't draw blood.

So, the reality is that acting is both pleasurable and painful. Creativity is both pleasurable and painful. (I'm not even getting into critics.) Accept the fact that if you are doing your work correctly, taking the necessary risks, you'll get more pleasure from the process and that pleasure in process is the point. What you are feeling is natural and productive but bring some Band-Aids.

25. Surviving the audition

Ah, a new season of plays! The actor is awash in dreams. Hope fills each Thespian like a nagging allergy. No, that's not right... Hope fills the air like moths drawn to an open flame! Definitely not it.

Anyway, hope fills the air. A season has been posted that runs the gamut from dear old *Hamlet* to *Jesus Christ Superstar,* and the actor longs for his or her breakout performance. Only one problem: the auditions. Preparing for the auditions. Surviving the auditions with our fragile dreams intact. The script—that's what we should be looking at, right? How do we get a line on what the director wants? How do we unlock the text so we can enter the nirvana of performance?

Okay, here's the user's guide.

Just read it. Don't imagine yourself in it. Don't salivate over the moment when you go down to the kitchen in the dead of night and find your mother drinking blood out of a teacup and realize she's a vampire. Just read it and let the story do its work on you.

Good, you did it. Now read it again—same drill—no counting your lines or imagining your costume. This second time you begin to realize *how* the story works and how it creates its impact. But you're still not in it. Here's the bad news: you have to read it once more. Okay, take the day off, but definitely do it tomorrow while the first two readings linger in your mind. Having a hard time getting down to reading it a third time? Have your boyfriend read it to you at the beach wearing a Speedo while you eat mango ice cream.

The good news is that during this third reading you're allowed to finally possess the role you want. The story is in you. You get the story. Now listen carefully (while finishing your mango) to how your character unfolds and functions. You're now asking yourself two questions as Speedo man reads: 1) Why, story-wise, does my character need to be in the scene? 2) Does my character win or lose in the scene?

Don't make a big deal of it. Just let the questions sit inside you while you listen (or read).

Congratulations. You have finished level one and can move on to level two. The level of difficulty ramps up a little, right? Now go through the script and pick out your character's most important relationships with others. A small part probably has one relationship and a large part probably has three to five. What does your character want from each of these relationships?

Pull out your trusty bound notebook (the secret to all acting success) and write down the key relationships: Hamlet/Ophelia, Hamlet/Gertrude, Hamlet/Claudius, Hamlet/Laertes, Hamlet/Horatio. Write down your answer to the above question. This will be crucial in your audition. Put a star by it so if they request you to read a Harnlet/Ophelia scene, you have a thought about it. Important: at this stage, don't just think about your character, think about your character relationships.

Onward and upward! You're at level three. Answer this question: what three characteristics are important in this character? Sort of in this vein: he is revengeful, confused, and depressed. She is jealous, shrewd, and funny. He is sexy, dominating, and selfish. She is ambitious, logical, and shy. You get the idea, so do it. You're not stuck with these characteristics. You could change them tomorrow or add a fourth. But right now, use your top three choices. Now, go through your character's scenes and see how these characteristics might inform those scenes, The key scenes, mind you—not the one where she feeds her English bulldog.

Surprisingly enough, your creativity is probably engaged by now and you are beginning to get excited by the possibility of getting the part and doing the role. Good. You need to care about this audition, and that caring gives you the energy to keep working.

Sidebar: does all of this seem like too much work? Guess what, there are forty other people auditioning for the role. Do you actually want this part or are you simply doing a little fantasizing?

Level four, continued. Okay. Now get down to work on the audition itself. Either you've been given the audition scenes or you're guessing what they will be or you're just supposed to do a general audition piece.

Option A. You're just supposed to do a general audition piece and the fools will cast from that. Remember where you wrote down three qualities you think the character possesses? Do an audition piece where you can apply those qualities. Does it seem that the pieces you have can't use those qualities (though you'll be surprised how many can)? Get a new piece. Write yourself a piece. Do a piece from the show.

You've been given the scene they want you to read. Better. Go back to your thoughts about the relationships. Use them in the scene. Have an agenda in the scene: how does my character want this scene to turn out? Does my character win or lose (play that)? Get those three qualities on the stage. And know the lines! If you really want the part then know the lines!

They are going to ask you to audition for the play, but the sadomasochists in charge haven't told you which scenes. Prepare what you think is the coolest scene your character has. Also prepare your character's funniest or most emotional scene. Three times out of four those are the scenes they'll ask for. If you've guessed wrong, be brave, say you'd really like to do a different scene (one you have prepared) and most times, they'll let you.

The last necessity: two days before the audition go back and read the whole play twice. Yes, twice, Twice in the same day. You are ready to generate ideas that result in good acting. You are really, really ready. You have enough information about the part and play to come away from these final two readings with some great ideas to include in your audition. I guarantee the ideas will come!

All right, this is, I know, a lot of work, but do you want a part or do you not? If you haven't really prepared then you have no realistic right to feel badly if you aren't cast. You don't. Period. Good auditions are a direct response to the script and role. Let your creative response to the text be the audition. Of course (sorry), that means you'll have to actually read the text four or five times if you truly, actually, no kidding, no fantasies, no shortcuts, no fooling yourself, want the role. Because it's a new season of plays! A fresh start! A new you! Hope fills the actor like…oh, never mind.

Hope won't get you the part, but the text will. Open the play and begin to read.

26. Competitive spirit

Is acting competitive? This is a useful and even important question that pops up in different forms in my classes. I think you know the answer, but you may not act on it. The larger answer is that when you are doing a play, a film, or a television segment, it isn't (in most cases). It should be, and almost always is, a cooperative art form. All the actors are harnessed to the script and working together to deliver it in a creative and responsible way, right? Right. Are there strange and bizarre exceptions? Oh, yeah. Strange, but true.

A well-known film actor has been known to step on the foot of the person he's working with to distract them during the take. I have seen an actor who was seated at a table notice an actor upstage playing with the window curtains during one of his important speeches, rise, and take that actor by the arm and walk him away from the window while continuing the speech. I have seen a performance where an actress turned to another performer playing with a white handkerchief during a scene, broke out of the text, and firmly said, "Stop that!"

These events are very rare—sort of like a birder seeing a magnolia warbler in North Carolina. They are, statistically, hardly worth mentioning. One of the grand things about acting is the cooperative nature of performance. Performance is usually the gorgeous act of humans working toward shared goals. Would that the rest of the world worked that way. So, no, you don't need a competitive nature to do the work.

However, you do have to get the part, and a good many other people want it just as badly as you do. Out in the world, this not only has an artistic component, but also affects your career and ability to make car payments. Does this turn acting into cage fighting? No. It is obviously not a matter of doing physical harm. Is there an indisputable score as in lacrosse, basketball, and volleyball? Nope. Is it more like figure skating? Maybe. There is creative scoring by the judges that is partly subjective and partly objective. Is figure skating competitive? Obviously. There are winners and losers. Is that true in auditions? Yes, there are winners and losers. Does a competitive nature assist in auditioning as it does in figure skating? Undeniably so. If you don't have a competitive nature, does it harm your chances in the biz? Yes.

Now, as in figure skating, there are subjective scores in play in the competitive world of auditions, the worst of which would probably be, "Does this actor have the look I want for the role?" In a lot of other workplaces you could take the employer who uses this measure to court. Is the idea of a look socially unevolved? Heck yes! Is it in play in the audition? Heck yes! Maybe in a hundred years it won't be. We live in hope.

Are you fit? I would say that, in the undergraduate acting program where I used to teach, less than 30 percent of the students hit the gym. In my professional work, I would say that at least 90 percent of actors and actresses under fifty do. Does this have a competitive component? Let's just say that actors get cast more often if they work to be fit.

All right, let's get back to the audition. What are the categories you are being compared to other auditioners in? Here are a few in no particular order:

1. Does your mind engage your body so that it moves and gestures in ways appropriate to the role? To put it more

simply, do you move or do you stand there like a tree? The people who are best at this do very well in auditions.

2. Do you have a voice and articulations that I can stand to listen to for two hours? There isn't necessarily positive scoring in this area, but there is absolutely negative scoring.

3. Are you charming or riveting? The scoring is widely subjective, but it's there.

4. Are you believable? The actor has a lot of control in this area.

5. Do you understand the text? Are you delivering what the text needs? This is where the game is won or lost given a decent score in the dreaded look category and the obvious fact that you don't stand there like a tree.

6. Is there a spontaneity in your work and thought appropriate to the given situation or do you sound like a recording?

If you don't score decently in these areas, if you don't stay up late and work and practice until you do, the odds are you won't get cast.

We can argue that the will necessary to improve in these areas could be called competitive. For me, it's a no-brainer — it is. I have a good friend who is a ping-pong hustler. He plays the game at ping-pong parlors for money. He spent the last two years improving his backhand by paying people to hit his backhand an hour and a half a day. Is this simply self-improvement or is it a competitive nature? Who cares? He claims it has doubled his income.

Do you have that will and instinct in your acting? In the professional world there will be people auditioning for the same role you are who, unless you are ready to rock, will have out-prepared you. Does that mean they will get the part? I don't know. How does it work out in figure skating? Do you have a guess?

Will you work an hour a day to improve your backhand? Is that an example of a competitive nature? Can't say, but today, an actor who wants the same part you do is practicing her backhand. Are you?

27. Shakespearean acting for philistines

Ah yes, Shakespeare! The great white whale that ate all the other great classic plays we never get to see. All right, all right, he wrote more undeniably great plays than any other playwright. Let's be generous and say he wrote a dozen. He also wrote a slew of middling plays and some turkeys.

I mean really, do you want to sit through *Timon of Athens* or *Henry VIII* when you could see Moliere's *Misanthrope* or Euripides' *Medea?* No you don't, but you have to because there are more than a hundred Shakespeare festivals in America and (as far as I know) not a single Moliere festival, plus endless college productions and high school productions of our beloved Bard. I personally have seen fourteen productions of *Romeo and Juliet* in my life and every one of them was boring after Mercutio died.

Let's say, for the sake of argument, that there are a hundred other classic plays written before the nineteenth century as good as Shakespeare's best. Why do we have to be eternally stuck with Willie's? It's like going nowhere but Starbucks for a cup of coffee. The guy is a road hog. Can't we please lay on the horn until he lets us pass?!

Plus the legions of Shakespeare scholars, fan girls, and acting teachers feed off the poor guy like suckerfish on whales and sharks. He isn't a playwright, he's an industry. Which brings us to acting Shakespeare, which you're not allowed to do unless you know the secret handshake. Thus if you don't study scansion from the cradle to the grave and mind your plosives, you will be bullied like a middle school kid with an accent There are people (nine of them) who go to Shakespeare to bask like sunning snakes in the poetry and the maze-like history and the endlessly praised imagery, while the millions are just hoping for some cool characters in a good story.

In the dozen or so great plays he wrote, that's what he delivers. And so, young actor, should you. As you're unlikely to get a job at your local Euripides Festival, here are a few ways to improve your Shakespeare work enough to get into the industry and start practicing the magic spells sold by the purists at their lemonade stands.

1. I recently followed a couple I had been seated next to who had been discussing politics and films at the intermission of *Love's Labour's Lost* at a major theatre that shall remain nameless. As they left, the woman said to the man, "I did not understand one single word they said." Other than that, they seemed quite pleased with the experience.

   Now, I have spent some time teaching acting in a B.F.A. program, and when I did the necessary audition class in which you are thrown from the roof if you don't have "a Shakespeare piece," the problem was much the same. The students have practically no idea what they are saying, but it's clear the scansion and iambic pentameter are in place. What to do? Here's what.

   Sit down by candlelight in your horrific dorm room and translate your piece from *Troilus and Cressida* into simple, clear, contemporary English. As you know, all Shakespeare editions have notes either on the facing page or bottom of the page explaining impenetrable phrases, but in your candlelit room you will need three or four editions to figure everything out. By the way, you won't have that problem with

Moliere, which is probably why they won't let him have a festival. Anyway, when you have turned the piece into understandable colloquial English (warning: do not let any Shakespeare scholars into your candlelit room) you now memorize the piece as you wrote it and rehearse it as if it was a real human talking about stuff real humans talk about in real situations. Then you perform it a bunch of times for anyone who will listen. So far, so good.

Now you go back and learn the lines to your audition piece just as Willie wrote it back in the day when people talked funny. Good. Now, here's the trick: you act the piece in *exactly the same way as you did when you understood it!* Amazingly, except for a couple of things I'm going to tell you in a minute, it's now almost good enough to get you cast in a small part in *Henry VI Part 2* (a really boring play) at the Okefenokee Shakespeare Festival and Bakery, playing in the theatre where the Moliere Festival should be. Why? Because you're no longer acting in a language you don't speak and you can say it like you mean it. This is philistine Shakespeare at its best.

2. There are a couple more things you ought to keep in mind to become a philistine immortal in the endless world of Shakespeare auditions. You shouldn't take any pauses except teeny tiny ones where there is a comma and itsy bitsy ones where there is a period. Because a lot of the sentences are too long, you have to figure out exactly (the breath score) where to take a really quick breath to get through the sentence. If you take any other pauses I will personally fly out to where you are and yell at you. One thing—if you take a pause either before or after "and" or "but" your ears will fall off and you will get a full body rash. That's about it except you have to be careful not to lose vocal energy on the last three

words of every sentence because then they will know you are an American and everybody knows Americans can't act Shakespeare.

3. Oh, I suppose you will need some blocking, so here is blocking that works for any and all Shakespeare audition pieces. Start the piece sitting in a chair. At the end of the fourth sentence, stand up. After a few more sentences, walk around behind the chair. One sentence before the end of your piece, put your hands on the back of the chair. Say the last sentence as you walk off the stage. Works like a charm every time.

If you really want to make some big money doing Shakespeare later on—full plays, not just audition pieces—you will have to study scansion and imagery for years! Of course you can avoid that if you and your friends start a Moliere Festival, which is a lot more fun and the costumes are better.

28. Charisma

I want to write about the actor's charisma, but I'm also sure I don't fully understand it.

It is however, crucial to the actor's success. If the actor has this charisma, there are many things that can be taught that will make the charisma more functional in storytelling. For instance, text analysis. Text analysis helps the actor do what he or she must do to make the story both clear and interesting. Text analysis asks questions like: how does this story work? What must I do to make my part of it function to reveal the whole?

But let's get back to the charisma itself.

Every fall for several years, I taught a beginning acting class for incoming freshmen at a small arts college. I would start by asking to see an audition piece. About 20 percent of the class (thus four out of the twenty) are much more interesting to watch and listen to than the others. They command attention and seem unafraid to do this work in front of others. They have a charisma that distinguishes them. They are, in this introductory audition piece, the "best." Over the course of four years and a lot of teaching, almost everyone in that original class of twenty improves. But the four who were the best to begin with are still the best. Their charisma still distinguishes them, even though they and the others now have more technique and understanding.

This brings up a key question: Can you teach it, if it isn't there originally? Well, I can't.

Let me break down what I would call the elements of charisma. I've tried this before, and I still can't say with confidence which are the most important except for "Yeah, sure I'll get up and act. It doesn't seem that scary." This lack of fear and open pleasure in acting seems central. Can this part of charisma be learned? Yeah... sort of.

Other parts of the actor's charisma—and you seem to need a combination of them to be charismatic—include the following.

1. A good or interesting voice
2. An energy that commands attention
3. An ability to think about what you say while you are saying it
4. A fairly large physical vocabulary
5. A sense of humor
6. An ability to feel as well as understand the situation you are in
7. An attractiveness: external, internal, or both
8. A pleasure in acting, enjoyment
9. Welcoming eyes (I can't explain this, but some actors invite you in and others don't)
10. Reactions that are recognizable but surprising
11. A sense they would like you or be interested in you.
12. An ability to connect one thing in a situation to another

Now, some of these I can teach you (at least a little) and some I can't. And that's the irony in teaching acting and the irony in your wishing to be taught. Until 1930, very few actors were taught. The teaching amounted to doing a lot of acting and learning from doing. My father, Victor Jory, who was in 135 films and some 400 plays, including nine on Broadway, and innumerable television and radio dramas, never took a single acting class. But he had big-time charisma.

He naturally had no fear of acting and (check the list) he excelled at numbers 1, 2, 4, 5, 7, 8, 9, and 11. If I had had him in class, I could have improved his thought process, his ability to feel inside a situation, the recognizable sense of his reactions, and his ability to connect one thing to another. That's only five out of twelve. The seven parts of charisma he had naturally allowed him a fifty-year career.

I take from this that only certain things can be taught. Now, we can call it charisma or talent, but the fact is that there are parts of charisma that, if you don't have them naturally, teaching can't teach even if you take acting class morning, noon, and night.

This takes me back to that first audition piece you do for me. If you don't really like to get up and act, don't have either physical or mental energy, a sense of humor, an internal or external attractiveness, a relatability or a pleasure in acting, then I can probably still help you—but probably not enough.

That may make you feel bad, but over the years I've come to believe it's a fact. I'm not sure what to do about this or what exactly my responsibility is. If I really acted on this idea and told people they lacked charisma and they were unlikely to have a career, then there wouldn't be enough acting students for me to have a job.

I know there's a logical fallacy in here somewhere. Let's just not think about it.

29. Artist-in-waiting

Can we please, please stop using the term "artist?" Well, okay, if we agree that anyone who wants to be an actor is, by definition, an artist, then so be it. It's like all crane operators are crane operators, right? If that's the deal, I buy it, but let's have a show of hands.

On the other hand, if an artist is something different than the above—if the title relates to some kind of defined hierarchy—then high school acting students appearing in *Zombie: The Musical* who describe themselves as "artists" need a talking to. Furthermore, if every actor, director, and acting teacher isn't an artist, what's the definition? I have a good idea: let's avoid this whole problem, because it's just a sucking swamp and it gets unbelievably illogical and self-serving and irritating. Even calling ourselves "theatre workers" or "film workers" or something you think of that doesn't imply hierarchy remains undefined.

See, my worry is that actors have so little real status in our country that we just call ourselves "artists" to make ourselves feel better, but it's a really pretentious name for an aspirin. Personally—and I have no real way to make a rational case for this definition—I'm in favor of thinking the term "artist" defines the very, very, very few in any generation who, through sheer talent or brilliant theory, have actually transformed our thought or practice as a whole.

Truth to tell, I find this personally painful, because it definitely leaves me out. If I were to take a guess at how many actors, directors, or teachers would actually get to wear the T-shirt in any generation, I'd guess a maximum of six. Maybe that leaves you out, too. But so that fistfights don't break out in our middle schools and award banquets, can't we just stop? It just makes us sound well, silly and pretentious.

I think what we do as actors, directors, designers, and technicians is completely justified and socially useful, so that running around like the Prince of Moldavia with a bunch of bogus medals on our chest that look like a fruit salad just isn't necessary. We tell the stories that need telling, period.

All our historical wise persons seem to agree that humility becomes us and creates the empathy we so desperately need. If they're right, let's get some. To come clean, I base more of this on the feeling I get when I apply that term to myself and feel, well, unrecognizable. I'm proud I can direct a play that entertains, perhaps enlightens, and makes its point. I don't need the selfie that "artist" implies. Not that anyone else really cares. I'm just aware of undefinable unease.

Luckily, the best acting seems to acknowledge that language is a very, very imprecise means of communication, and so is self-image. I sort of agree with the ideas behind "Just do it." My waiter the other night seemed to have a lot of presence and panache, so on an impulse I asked if he was an actor, and he answered, "Artist-in-waiting." Clever and possibly true. The pear-walnut salad, by the way, could have been called "artistic." Or maybe it was just a really good pear salad.